ROBERT PATTINSON
THE BIOGRAPHY

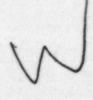

ROBERT PATTINSON
THE BIOGRAPHY

SARAH OLIVER

Published by John Blake Publishing Ltd,
3 Bramber Court, 2 Bramber Road,
London W14 9PB, England

www.johnblakebooks.com

www.facebook.com/johnblakebooks [f]
twitter.com/jblakebooks [t]

This edition published in 2015

ISBN: 978 1 78418 603 6

British Library Cataloguing-in-Publication Data:

A catalogue record for this book is available from the British Library.

Design by www.envydesign.co.uk

Printed in Great Britain by CPI Group (UK) Ltd

1 3 5 7 9 10 8 6 4 2

Papers used by John Blake Publishing are natural, recyclable products made
from wood grown in sustainable forests. The manufacturing processes conform to
the environmental regulations of the country of origin.

Every attempt has been made to contact the relevant copyright-holders,
but some were unobtainable. We would be grateful if the appropriate people
could contact us.

Dedicated, with love, to Hayley, Kyri and Emily

ABOUT THE AUTHOR

Sarah Oliver is from Widnes in Cheshire. She was the author of *Robert Pattinson A–Z*, which was a hit worldwide. She also wrote the double biography of Harry Styles and Niall Horan, *One Direction A–Z*, which was a *Sunday Times* Best Seller, and *Taylor Lautner A–Z*.

She has written over 700 articles on Robert and knows more about him than any other journalist on the planet; her work on all things Rob has been viewed by over 10 million.

Why not follow Sarah – @SarahOliverAtoZ – on Twitter?

CONTENTS

CHAPTER 1

1986 – A STAR IS BORN

When Rob Pattinson opens his eyes first thing in the morning and wipes the sleep from them, it can take him a while to figure out where he is. He might be sprawled across his bed in his Los Angeles mansion, or in a luxury hotel suite virtually anywhere in the world.

He has come so far since *Twilight* catapulted him to stardom on 17 November 2008, the night of the Los Angeles premiere. His life took a turn that no one could have expected, not least his parents, Richard and Clare...

Rob's parents will always remember the day he entered their lives, 13 May 1986. He was born in a private clinic close to Barnes, London, and they gave him the name Robert Thomas Pattinson. They already had two daughters, Lizzy and Victoria, but he was their first son. He was the missing piece of the Pattinson jigsaw puzzle and his arrival completed their little family.

Back then, they might have thought that the little boy in their arms would grow up to live not far from them, maybe get a job in London, pop home at weekends for a roast dinner or to simply catch up on things.

They wouldn't have thought in a million years that he would end up being a world-famous actor living in Los Angeles, thousands of miles from them. If they want to see him, outside of FaceTime or Skype, then they have to pop on a plane and make the trip to his LA home or to his latest filming location.

The Pattinsons have always been a close-knit group of people. Even if they can't see each other on a day-to-day basis, as a family they always try to be together for special occasions. For instance, when Rob turned twenty-three while he was filming *New Moon* in Vancouver, Canada, his family made the trip over to see him and enjoyed a special celebratory meal out with him and his cast mates. His family mean the world to him and he always tries to make spending Christmas with them a priority.

Richard and Clare raised Rob and his sisters in a semi-detached five-bedroomed Victorian house in Barnes, south-west London. Barnes is an affluent Thames-side village, with a cricket green, rugby club, bookshop, delis, boutiques and restaurants. It is also the location of one of the most famous music studios in London – The Olympic Sound Studios.

2

Famous bands like the Rolling Stones, Oasis and The Arctic Monkeys have all recorded tracks there.

Rob's parents might have been wealthy but they didn't want Rob and his sisters to grow up spoilt. Even now, they expect him to be humble and find it strange when they visit him on the sets of his movies and his assistants ask him if he would like something to eat or drink. They think he should get things for himself, rather than relying on others.

Richard and Clare are retired now but when Rob was growing up they both worked. His dad was a taxi driver and sold vintage cars and his mum was a booker at a modelling agency. She encouraged Rob to become a model when he was in his young teens but once he reached puberty, the work dried up. Rob jokes now that he stopped being in demand when he 'stopped looking like a girl.'

He told *Look* magazine: 'I never did any sport, so I was always the kind of gangly guy.'

Lizzy and Victoria loved having a young brother to play with and when he was really young, they would dress him up and call him 'Claudia'. They were overprotective of him when he was growing up and are still quite wary of new people who join his friendship group.

All the Pattinson children have taken creative career paths – Lizzy is a singer-songwriter and Victoria works in advertising/marketing. Victoria helps brands develop creative ideas and works on their social media and PR strategies. They are both based in London.

Lizzy is becoming more famous in her own right after appearing on the British version of *The X Factor* in 2014. She reached the Judges Houses' round and was almost picked by Simon Cowell to appear on the live shows. Although narrowly missing out was a big blow she vowed to continue singing and could very well apply for *The X Factor* again in the future.

DID YOU KNOW?

Before Lizzy became passionate about singing she was a budding actress and appeared in several plays. Lizzy was also in the short film *Mood Swing* (2007), which was produced with a budget of £500. She played the part of Gemma, girlfriend of the main character Ewan. The plot in short is that the couple are threatened by a man and narrowly escape with their lives.

Lizzy has always been a keen dancer and has a Grade 8 in ballet. When she was at college she did gigs in pubs and clubs in London. After she finished her A-levels she was approached and asked if she would like to join the electronic dance music group Aurora. Lizzy jumped at the chance and was thrilled when their two singles, 'Dreaming' and 'The Day It Rained Forever', made the Top Twenty charts in the UK. They toured all around the UK, Europe and North America and even managed to land No. 1 on the Billboard Dance Charts after collaborating with Milk & Sugar on their track 'Let The Sunshine In'. It was a wonderful opportunity and made Lizzy feel like becoming a singer professionally was a real possibility.

DID YOU KNOW?

Lizzy was given the opportunity to sing ambient background vocals for the Carter Burwell track 'Who Are They?' for the *Twilight* soundtrack. It's the track that plays when Bella sees the Cullens for the first time in the cafeteria.

She confided to *Cellar Door* magazine: 'I recorded the vocals with Carter Burwell and Catherine Hardwicke at Hans Zimmer's studio in Los Angeles and Air Studios in London. They were both such amazing people to work with and it was fascinating to see and hear how much the music affects the mood of the scene. I feel honoured to have been a part of the film, albeit a very small part. It was so much fun.'

Lizzy and Victoria look very similar and it can be hard to distinguish between the two. When Rob first became famous the paparazzi would sometimes photograph them leaving places with him and the next day their faces would be plastered all over Internet sites, with bloggers claiming to have found Rob's secret girlfriend.

Rob and his sisters are very well spoken and this is not by

accident. Rob confessed to *The Inquirer*: 'My parents were just very aware of how you're treated differently in the world if you speak articulately, so it was just the way I was brought up.'

Rob is a huge dog lover and he has always been fascinated by them. He admitted to *Gala.de* that if he had to choose one animal to be, he would pick a dog. He said: 'You sleep, sit around, get stroked, eat and get walked from time to time. That's great. There is a deep connection between me and dogs.'

While growing up, his West Highland Terrier Patty was the member of his family he was closest to. When *myfoxphilly.com* asked him about his love life in 2008, Rob joked: 'My dog is the only lady friend in my life. I have a really girly dog, but she hasn't got a girly attitude. My dog is a little bit like Beyoncé – it has a Beyoncé walk, which is strange for a little terrier.'

He was absolutely devastated in 2009 when Patty passed away and admitted to *Parade* a year later: 'I keep talking about my dog all the time. It was an incredible dog, and I said in an interview recently she was the most important person in my life.

'My family went crazy with me for saying that. But, however ridiculous it may seem to some people, my relationship with my dog was a defining moment. Having the dog die was, literally, like the worst day of my life. It was like losing a family member.'

Rob spent a lot of time with Patty when he was growing up

because he didn't have lots of friends. He was pretty introverted and liked spending time on his own. He had a really happy childhood in Barnes, but admitted to *Empire*: 'I didn't have very many toys – I just used to play with a pack of cards all the time. I'd pretend the cards were other things. I liked any toy that didn't involve playing with other children.'

His parents wanted him to have the best start in life so enrolling him in good schools was a priority. Rob's first school was Tower House Preparatory and to send a child there today would cost around £11,000 a year. It's an independent boys-only establishment for pupils aged four to thirteen in East Sheen, south-west London. *The Good Schools Guide 2014* praises its old-fashioned qualities: 'Little boys, tongues out in concentration, painstakingly perfecting their Ps and Qs, is a heart-warming sight.'

Rob revealed in an interview with *The Sunday Times*: 'I wasn't with the cool gang, or the uncool ones. I was transitional, in between. I was never a leader, and the idea of my ever being made head boy would have been a complete joke. I wasn't involved in much at school and I was never picked for any of the teams. I wasn't at all focused at school and I didn't achieve much.'

In fact Rob and his sisters were encouraged by their parents to get small jobs as soon as they were old enough so they could understand the meaning of money. Richard and Clare didn't want them to grow up spoilt. Rob became a bit of a dog walker for a friend of his mother's and his sister Lizzy got herself a Saturday job at the local library. After he turned ten, Rob become a paper boy and started delivering newspapers around Barnes. He was paid around £10 a week, which was a lot of money for boy of his age.

When Rob was twelve he left the Tower House Preparatory. He hasn't ever revealed in interviews exactly why he left, perhaps his grades weren't good enough.

Richard and Clare decided to move Rob to the Harrodian School, which was less pressured. It was only founded in 1993, but children still had to have an interview and pass entrance exams to gain a place there.

Rob found having girls in his classes a novelty to begin with as his last school had been all boys. As time went by he found being with girls on a daily basis had a big impact on his daily life and he had his first kiss when he was twelve. He told *Newsround*: 'I became cool and discovered hair gel.'

When he was fourteen, Rob and two of his friends decided to form a rap group. He confessed to *The New York Times*: '[It was] pretty hardcore for three private-school kids from suburban London.' They used to have practice sessions at Rob's house but they didn't get much privacy. 'And my mum's like, cramping our style, popping her head in to ask, "You boys want a sandwich?"'

It wasn't just rap that Rob was interested in, he was passionate about all different types of music. He figured that he'd end up an old man in a bar, playing the piano and supping whisky every night as he played his favourite pieces. He felt so alive when he was playing the piano and couldn't see himself ever tiring of it.

> **DID YOU KNOW?**
> Rob did get bullied at school but he didn't let the bullies win. One day someone stole the shoelaces from his shoes, but he just carried on wearing them and they became his trademark.

Rob was very untidy, both at home and at school. So much so his mum used to despair. In one school newsletter he was described as the 'runaway winner of last term's Form Three untidy desk award'. He much preferred playing computer games or watching *Doctor Who*, *Sharky & George* or *Hammertime* on his TV than tidying his room.

CHAPTER 2

TRYING TO FIND HIS JULIET

Rob was quite a shy teenager and he found it difficult to approach girls he was attracted to. He used to try to make them laugh by using chat-up lines, his favourite being, 'Will you marry me? I don't want to mess around!' He would also sit next to girls he fancied and tell them, 'I just got out of prison' just to see the look of terror in their eyes. His awkwardness made him appreciate when a girl approached him instead, as it meant he didn't have to worry about being rejected.

And back then Rob liked girls who were a bit crazy and enjoying chasing young women who played hard to get, but this meant that he struggled to find any who wanted a lasting relationship with him. The girls that he did briefly date had to make do with cheap dates, as his modelling and paper-round money didn't stretch far. He just about managed to scrape enough cash to take one girl to Cornwall for the weekend, but that was only after he got the train tickets for free and in the event they had to stay somewhere cheap and nasty.

Cinema dates were a big no-no for Rob because he tended to overanalyse films and point out their flaws, which wasn't exactly what his dates wanted. He took one girl to the zoo but couldn't afford the entrance fee so they had to run around the outside fence instead. It started to rain, but Rob thought it was romantic.

Rob has never wanted to conform and when it came to deciding what he wanted to do when he left school he knew he didn't want a boring job. He dreamed about being a political speech-writer but changed his mind when he realised what it would involve. He told the *Los Angeles Times*: 'I just liked the whole idea of it. I wanted to be involved with politics, that's what my whole plan was. I was going to go to university and then I just thought, "Ah, I can't be bothered to do anything!" [laughs]. I don't want to do any more homework!'

Rather than think about his long-term future Rob just wanted a girlfriend. He found not being able to get female attention at school quite frustrating at times, admitting to *Glamour Spanish* magazine: 'The ones I liked hated me and the ones that liked me were not my type. But that's something that I still go through – I like girls that I shouldn't like. But I'm learning and now I take my time before I let the girl know.'

In some respects, if Rob hadn't struggled to get a girlfriend while he was at school he might never have taken up acting. His dad wouldn't have felt the need to suggest he join the local drama club if Rob had had a steady girlfriend. Rob explained to the *Daily Mail*: 'It's all a bit of a surprise, the acting and fame. I never did acting in school. My dad was in a restaurant and saw a bunch of pretty girls and decided to go up and ask where they had been. They said they went to this drama club, so he said we'd better go down too! It's the only time he's done something like that. We went down there and I began to work backstage. Then one day I was the only one left to play a leading role. That was the first acting I'd done and yet somehow I got an agent.'

The drama club in question was The Barnes Theatre Club. It was a professionally run studio theatre that had been providing the people of Barnes and West Molesey with great plays to go and watch for over thirty years. It was the perfect place for fifteen-year-old Rob to start his acting career and he would go on to make some great friends during his time with the company. He explained to Scholastic Corporation how he made the jump from backstage to a performing role: 'Rusty and Ann, who are the directors, were actors themselves and were very talented. They were a very good group, and for some reason when I finished the backstage thing, I just decided that

I should try to act. So I auditioned for *Guys and Dolls* and got a little tiny part as some Cuban dancer or something, and then in the next play I got the lead part, and then I got my agent. So I owe everything to that little club.'

> **DID YOU KNOW?**
>
> Rob met his good friend Tom Sturridge during his time with the company. Rob and Tom often went up against each other for the same parts, but they remain good friends to this day. Both managed to secure small roles together in Vanity Fair and Tom went on to play 'Young' Carl in The Boat That Rocked (2009). He was nominated for a prestigious Tony Award for his role in the Broadway play Orphans in 2013. He is engaged to actress Sienna Miller and they have a daughter, Marlowe.

Once Rob got an agent, the hard work really started. He had to audition for parts and work on becoming a better actor – as well as attending school. His agent started searching for television roles that would suit Rob but in the meantime he auditioned and won a part in a professional production of William Shakespeare's *Macbeth*. It was to be performed at The Old Sorting Office Community Arts Centre in Barnes, only a matter of minutes from his home, so location-wise it couldn't have been closer. He was playing the part of King Malcolm, who succeeds Macbeth to be the King of Scotland.

This was to be his first experience of performing to a large audience.

It must have been strange for Rob receiving standing ovations every night and then having to get up early the next day to go to school. Rob's favourite subject at the Harrodian School was English because his teacher really got him interested in writing and didn't mind marking his long, rambling answers that went on for pages and pages. With the school's encouragement, he developed a love of reading and this has continued throughout his adult life. He reads books that would be too heavy for the majority of people and enjoys watching non-mainstream films.

Rob loves reading a mixture of novels, poetry anthologies and memoirs. Here are some of his favourites:

Money by Martin Amis

Ticket to Ride by Dennis Potter

The Professionals by Owen Laukkanen

The Ballad of the Sad Café by Carson McCullers

My Friend the Mercenary: A Memoir by James Brabazon

The Brain That Changes Itself: Stories of Personal Triumph from the Frontiers of Brain Science by Norman Doidge

The Art of Struggle by Michel Houellebecq

Life by Keith Richards

Nine Stories by J D Salinger

The Fountainhead by Ayn Rand

Consider the Lobster by David Foster Wallace

2666: A Novel by Roberto Bolaño

Complete Poems by Charles Baudelaire

Doomed Love (Penguin Great Loves) by Virgil

Collected Short Stories by E M Forster

Independent People by Halldór Laxness

Kill Your Friends by John Niven

While Rob was at school, other subjects aside from English failed to capture his imagination and he struggled to motivate himself in lessons. In Rob's school reports his teachers commented that he didn't try very hard, which was disappointing for his parents. They were paying over £15,000 a year to send him to the school because they wanted him to get a good education and they were worried that he'd walk away with bad grades.

Rob confessed to the *Daily Mirror*: 'I wasn't very academic. My dad said to me, "Okay, you might as well leave since you're not working very hard." When I told him I wanted to stay on for my A-levels, he said I'd have to pay my own fees, then he'd pay me back if I got good grades.'

Thankfully, Rob was able to use his pay cheques from acting jobs to pay his school fees. He thought he'd be able to study really hard but he had to miss lots of classes because he was filming abroad and couldn't dedicate much time to revising.

To his amazement he managed to get excellent grades, an A and two Bs. His dad never did pay him back but Rob can't have minded too much.

Rob was determined to become a successful actor so didn't have an immediate plan to use his qualifications but knew that it was good to have them to fall back on, if need be. If he hadn't gotten into acting he thinks he would have liked to have become a music producer or a stockbroker. He would have loved the creative side of being in the music industry and the fast pace of being on the Stock Exchange floor.

DID YOU KNOW?
Rob did actually apply for university but didn't receive a single offer. This may have been because his expected grades were low at the time he applied, as you have to apply a year before you receive your A-level results.

CHAPTER 3

STARTING OUT

R ob felt a mixture of nerves and excitement on his first day on a movie set. He had successfully auditioned for the Mira Nair directed *Vanity Fair* and was to play Rawdy Crawley, the son of Reese Witherspoon's character, Becky Sharp.

He expressed how it felt to *MoviesOnline*: 'You turn up on set and I'd done one amateur play, and you kind of end up doing a film with Reese Witherspoon and you have a trailer and stuff. It was the most ridiculous thing. And I was thinking, "I should be an actor. I'm doing a movie with Reese Witherspoon." How is this happening?'

Filming took place in Bath, Gloucestershire and Kent during the summer of 2003 and the schedule was extremely tight as Reese was pregnant at the time. She went on to have her son Deacon on 23 October.

In July 2010, Reese reflected on what it was like to play Rob's mum. She told *Movies Online*: 'I remember he was verrrry handsome. I was like, "I have a really handsome son." I was supposed to play an older version of my character who had been sort of a ruined woman and was at the end of her life. I remember I just had to sob and cry all over him. He was great. He was a wonderful actor.'

> **DID YOU KNOW?**
> Rob would go on to play Reese's lover in the 2011 movie *Water for Elephants*.

Rob thoroughly enjoyed working with Reese and the rest of the cast. He couldn't have been happier when it was the premiere night on 16 August 2004. He was so looking forward to his friends and family seeing him on the big screen but alas, it wasn't to be. His scenes were cut and he didn't appear once during the cinema release of the movie. This was made more awkward because his flatmate Tom Sturridge was in the movie too and his scene was just before Rob's so they expected to see it right after Tom's scene but it wasn't to happen. Thankfully, he did appear in the DVD release so all was not lost.

Rob confessed to *The Irish Times*: 'It was my first real job. I went along to the premiere, but nobody had told me that I had been cut out. I didn't realise until the film ended. The casting agent was the same one who did *Harry Potter*. They felt so bad about it – they gave me an early meeting for the next *Harry Potter* film. And that went well.'

Vanity Fair wasn't a success in the box office. It cost more than it made, despite having Reese Witherspoon in the leading role. It received a score of 6.2 out of 10 from the Internet Movie Database (IMDb), based on 16,086 reviews. Stephen Holden from *The New York Times* wrote a lukewarm review of the movie. He commented: 'Her eyes snapping like tiny firecrackers and jutting her chin, Reese Witherspoon makes an appealingly crafty Becky Sharp in Mira Nair's bland but color-drenched adaptation of William Makepeace Thackeray's 1848 novel, *Vanity Fair*. Ms Witherspoon, as usual, conveys a bristly, determined spunk. But if her performance emits enough sparks to hold the screen, it never ignites a dramatic brush fire. Despite her make-do British accent, she is quintessentially American in attitude and body language, even more a fish out of water in *Vanity Fair* than she seemed in *The Importance of Being Earnest*.'

Movie critic Roger Ebert, however, loved the adaptation and gave it 4 out of 4 stars in his review, saying: 'Some of the film's best moments come when characters administer verbal flayings to one another. Matilde is unforgiving when she is crossed. But the most astonishing dialogue comes from a character named Lord Steyne (Gabriel Byrne), who Becky meets for the first time when she's a girl in her father's studio. Steyne fancies a portrait of Becky's mother; her father prices it at 3 guineas, but Becky insists on 10, putting on a good show of sentimental attachment to her departed parent. Now, many years later, Steyne crosses Becky's path again. She reminds him of their first meeting. It occurs to him that having purchased a portrait of the parent, he might purchase the original of the daughter. This sets up a dinner-table scene in the Steyne household at which the lord verbally destroys every member of his family, not sparing the rich mulatto heiress from the Caribbean who married his son for his title even though "the whole world knows he's an idiot."'

Although Rob must have felt a tad humiliated at the *Vanity Fair* premiere, looking back he must be glad about what happened because he landed the part of Cedric Diggory off the back of it. Luck was certainly on his side as he was the first to audition for the role, explaining, 'I was shooting another film in South Africa during the entire period of the casting process for *Goblet of Fire*. The casting agent had contacted my agent about seeing me for Cedric. Basically, I was able to get a meeting with Mike Newell and two of the casting directors the day before I left for South Africa to shoot this other movie. It was before anyone else had been seen for the other parts, so it was quite a cool position to be in.' Rob revealed to Scholastic Corporation, 'They did the rest of the casting for it afterwards. Then, the day I returned from South Africa, I got the callback and they told me in the audition that I had got the part.'

The movie that Rob had been filming in South Africa was *Ring of the Nibelungs*. Rob had learnt so much from filming *Vanity Fair* but *Ring of the Nibelungs* developed his acting skills even more, and had involved him living in South Africa for three-and-a-half months. To be only seventeen and living away from his family and friends must have been quite a challenge for Rob because he was used to his mum doing everything for him.

In the movie, Rob played the part of Giselher, younger brother of Princess Kriemhild (played by Alicia Witt) and King Gunther (played by Samuel West). The movie was based on Nordic legend and told the tale of a young blacksmith who slays a dragon and wins the heart of a warrior queen. It was a German made-for-television movie and had a budget of $23,000,000.

The movie might have been produced for a German audience but it was released internationally under different titles. These included *Dark Kingdom: The Dragon King*, *Curse of the Ring*, *Sword of Xanten* and *Die Nibelungen*. It first appeared on German TV screens in November 2004 but British audiences didn't get to see it until December 2005.

Ring of the Nibelungs received a score of 6.7 out of 10 from IMDb, based on 7,707 reviews. *DVD Talk*'s Scott Weinberg admitted that he quite enjoyed watching the movie in his review, writing: 'In Germany it's called *Die Nibelungen* and it ran three hours as a TV mini-series. In the UK it played theatrically under the title *The Sword of Xanten*. If you happen to be in South Africa (which is where the flick was shot), the title you'll want to remember is *The Curse of the Ring*.

'Here in the U.S. it's called *Dark Kingdom: The Dragon King*, and no matter what the flick's actual name is, the story is based on numerous ancient Nordic legends, including a few that helped inspire Tolkien to write *The Lord of the Rings*. Yep, it's a magic / dragons / swords / romance / treachery sorta thing, precisely like what you'll find in *Excalibur*, *Dragonslayer*, and ... um ... *Krull*.

'Provided you don't watch this type of movie for the acting performances, *Dark Kingdom* isn't a half-bad little time-waster. It's got lots of twists and turns, a few unintentionally amusing components, and a pretty darn nifty dragon battle. It's certainly not a great film, but hey, this is coming from a guy who proudly owns a copy of *The Sword and the Sorcerer* DVD, so maybe I'm just a sucker for the whole sword-swingin' sub-genre.'

Jamie Russell from the BBC gave the movie a feeble 2 out of 5 stars, saying: 'A Teutonic Tolkien cash-in light on brains, brawn and budget, *Xanten* is fantasy cinema at its least fantastic.

'Forget Wagner's rousing tale of passion and magic rings, this feels more like one of those disposable pulp novels to be found lining the shelves of the bookshop's fantasy section with gaudy covers that usually feature archaic symbols, scantily clad women and the odd elf. The dialogue's about as well-written ("Be patient child, Odin's powers are in the runes but they won't be rushed") and lead actor Fürmann is even more wooden than the Austrian Oak was when he last stepped into Conan The Barbarian's sandals.'

Jack Foley from *indieLondon* was equally damning of the Uli Edel directed movie: 'With so much mythology behind it, it's little wonder that *Sword of Xanten* clocks in at well in excess of two hours, but anyone expecting an epic to rival *The Lord of The Rings* is sure to be sorely disappointed. The movie is constantly hindered by a lacklustre script and some truly bland performances, which tests the patience long before the halfway stage. While the effects are not-so special as to leave viewers decidedly under-whelmed.'

CHAPTER 4

HELLO, HARRY

At eighteen years old, Rob got a small taste of the full-blown fame he would experience years later once *Twilight* was released. He had dreamed of becoming a professional actor but he had never imagined being given as big an opportunity as playing Cedric Diggory in *Harry Potter and the Goblet of Fire*.

When Rob had filmed his first two movies, *Vanity Fair* and *Ring of the Nibelungs*, he had still been at school, so he'd had to juggle his studies and being a professional actor on a film set. With *Harry Potter*, he had left school and could give acting his full attention.

The *Harry Potter* set was like nothing Rob had experienced before, as there were hundreds upon hundreds of people bustling around, so many crew, plus actors and extras. It had a budget of $150 million, which made the $23 million budgets for *Vanity Fair* and *Ring of the Nibelungs* seem like small change.

From Day One, he felt under immense pressure because his fellow actors had so much more acting experience than he had, and many had been in the three previous *Harry Potter* movies so they knew how things worked. He confessed to the BBC: 'On *Harry Potter* I was so conscious of the fact that I didn't know what I was doing, I used to sit on the side of the set, throwing up.'

Initially, he felt intimidated by Emma Watson (who played Hermione Granger), Daniel Radcliffe (Harry Potter) and Rupert Grint (Ron Weasley). He knew they were all experienced actors and this made him feel a bit inadequate. To get over his nerves, he pretended that he was someone else, not Rob from Barnes on his third proper acting job. He said he was twenty-four and from South Africa and instead of mixing with the other actors, he just sat around drinking coffee for the first month. He soon dropped the act, though, and enjoyed getting to know Emma and the rest of the cast.

While Rob wasn't sure if he had what it took to play Cedric convincingly, the movie's director Mike Newell had absolute faith in him and knew he was the right actor for the job. He told one reporter: 'Cedric exemplifies all that you would expect the Hogwarts' champion to be. Robert Pattinson was born to play the role – he's quintessentially English, with chiselled public-schoolboy good looks.'

Rob might have had the perfect looks to play Cedric, but he didn't have the right body to play him from the outset. Almost immediately after arriving on set, he was told he had to work on his fitness levels because his body didn't match up to how the producers envisaged Cedric's to be. Rob had never been into sport or fitness but the character he was to play was supposed to be ultra-fit. He admitted to the BBC: 'I hadn't done anything for about six months before so I was a little bit unfit. I remember the costume designer saying when I was trying on swimming trunks (for the merpeople task scenes) "Aren't you supposed to be fit, you could be playing a sissy poet or something."

'The next day I got a call from the assistant director about a personal training programme.'

He has since admitted: 'It was run by one of the stunt team, who are the most absurdly fit guys in the world. I can't even do ten press-ups! I did about three weeks of that and in the end, I think he got so bored of trying to force me to do it that he wrote it all down so that I could do it at home.'

Rob did attempt to follow the exercise plan at home but he hurt one of his shoulders so had to stop working out. By the time it came to shooting his scenes he might not have been as fit as the directing team would have liked but he was certainly a lot fitter than he had been on his first day on set.

His Triwizard Tournament scenes were very physically demanding so on days when they filmed those scenes Rob was left feeling exhausted. His maze scenes were particularly hard-going on his body because he was hit by hedges, swung around on ropes and had to run around and hit Daniel Radcliffe (who played Harry) again and again. He also had to learn to scuba dive and act at the same time, which was a huge challenge.

During filming, Rob carried a journal that he wrote in daily, pretending to 'be' Cedric. He felt writing as his character helped him understand more about Cedric and ultimately give a better performance. Rob confessed to *Entertainment Weekly*: 'It was my diary but it became more and more and more about requests to the "fates" – "I will do this, if you provide me with this." It sounds absolutely ridiculous, but I had so much faith in this little book. I remember one time I wrote, "Please don't give me all my luck now. Make it all stretch – I don't mind waiting. Make it stretch for seventy years."'

The movie was released on 18 November 2005 and topped box offices around the world for weeks. In total it made just under $900 million worldwide, making it the highest-grossing film of 2005.

At the premiere in London's Leicester Square, Rob was taken aback by the number of girls screaming his name. It was like nothing he'd ever experienced before. He had chosen not to go down the designer route when it came to his clothes and instead wore an oversized red velvet jacket he had bought from a charity shop and some black leather trousers.

> **DID YOU KNOW?**
> *The Times* named Rob their 2005 British Star of Tomorrow after the release of *Harry Potter and the Goblet of Fire*.

Harry Potter and the Goblet of Fire received a score of 7.6 out of 10 from IMDb, based on 332,799 reviews. *New York Times* reviewer Manohla Dargis declared: 'Childhood ends for Harry Potter, the young wizard with the zigzag scar and phantasmagorical world of troubles, not long after the dragons have roared and the merpeople have screeched their empty threats through broken teeth. And, as in the book, *Harry Potter and the Goblet of Fire* on which this latest and happily satisfying film adaptation is based, childhood ends with screams and a final shudder in a graveyard crowded with tombstones and evil. In a scene of startling intensity, one boy dies while another is delivered from the malevolent force that has steadily wended its way through J. K. Rowling's series toward its prey.

'Mr. Fiennes enters the film spectacularly, if regrettably late, whooshing into that crowded graveyard like a Butoh dancer from hell. He brings the film to an unsettling close, one that doesn't so much polish off the story as leave it in tatters.'

Stephanie Zacharek from *CINEMABLEND* wasn't blown away by the movie, writing: 'The same cast is back, but for *Goblet of Fire* Harry Potter gets a new director in the form of

Mike Newell. Mike's never directed a movie of this magnitude, and it shows. The film is well put together, and *Goblet of Fire* shines in smaller character moments like a school dance, but it's sometimes visually unimpressive. The school looks dreary and dark, sometimes rather bland. Dark can be good, but it's not very magical. The movie's long too, perhaps no longer than the others, but it feels longer. It drags, jumping between different sections it seems as though there's three movies in here instead of one.

'The Triwizard Tournament begins near the start of the film, and carries through to the end. It's being held at Hogwarts, and students from other schools have come to compete. New characters are introduced in an almost cursory way; most, with the exception of a fine young lad named Cedric (Robert Pattinson), are never developed.'

Rob remained humble, even after the success of the movie. He didn't get big-headed and was always honest about the people he actually got to know during filming and those he didn't. One of the actors he didn't get to know on a personal level was Oscar-winning actor Ralph Fiennes. He admitted to *GQ* magazine: 'I didn't really talk to Ralph Fiennes while I was doing *Harry Potter* and the only thing I did with him was when he stepped on my head. Then I went to this play and he was there. And this girl said, "You've worked with Ralph Fiennes, haven't you, Robert?" And I was like, "Well, no…" and

Ralph said, "Yes, I stepped on your head." And that was the extent of our conversation.'

Because Rob's character was killed off at the end of *Harry Potter and the Goblet of Fire* he didn't have the opportunity to film another *Harry Potter* movie, which was a real shame. David Yates, the director of the next movie, did, however, include a brief flashback in *Harry Potter and the Order of the Phoenix* (2007), which showed Rob as Cedric, much to fans' delight.

CHAPTER 5

LONDON CALLING

Playing Cedric had whetted Rob's appetite for big roles and he was determined to learn how to be an even better actor by the time he secured his next acting job. He decided that it was time to stand on his own two feet and moved out of his childhood home to live with his good friend Tom Sturridge in Soho, London.

The two budding actors rented a flat and had some unforgettable times together, just discovering who they were and figuring out the kind of lives they wanted to live. When Rob thinks about those days he can't help but smile. He told one journalist: 'It was so cool! You had to walk through a restaurant kitchen to get up to the roofs, but you could walk along all the roofs. I didn't do anything for a year, I just sat on the roof and played music – it was like the best time I ever had.'

It was during this time in his life when he met Nina Schubert, his first love. The blonde-haired, blue-eyed model was Rob's neighbour and they would date for three years before splitting. Rob never reveals her name in interviews but shared with *Glamour* magazine: 'It's weird to enjoy your first love, especially if the relationship lasts a long time. Our relationship was really beautiful, but we didn't have an obsessive love [like in *Twilight*]. Her presence in my life made me very happy for three years. Now it's kind of hard to talk about it.'

DID YOU KNOW?

Nina gave up being a model because she didn't think the lifestyle of a model was particularly healthy and moved to New Zealand, where she worked at a freezing works, sorting out boned-out meat because it was well paid. In her spare time she paints and Rob actually commissioned her to do a painting for him in 2009.

Rob won a part in Roland Schimmelpfennig's *The Woman Before* at the Royal Court Theatre in London but he was fired before opening night. 'I don't know why I was fired. They probably said something, but I was so furious I wasn't even listening,' he confessed to *The Hollywood Reporter*.

He didn't do any more theatre and instead focused on television. He was cast in the 2006 TV drama *The Haunted*

Airman for the BBC. Rob played the lead role of Toby – a pilot who returns home from World War II to be confined to a wheelchair (he is looked after by an aunt and a psychiatrist). The drama was based on the 1948 Dennis Wheatley novel, *The Haunting of Toby Jugg*, and is extremely dark. Toby is haunted by an evil, ghost-like presence and thinks he is losing his mind.

Rob really couldn't have picked a part more different than that of Cedric, and really had to put a lot of effort into understanding how Toby would feel, returning home from war as an invalid. In 2009 he told one interviewer: 'My best acting experience was *The Haunted Airman* for BBC2. I play a World War Two pilot, who gets shot and paralysed. He gets terrible shellshock and basically goes insane. It's a great part. I was in a wheelchair all the time, which is always good, just chain-smoking throughout the entire film.'

The Haunted Airman received a score of 4.8 out of 10 from IMDb, based on 1,554 reviews. *DVD Talk's* Justin Felix didn't feel Toby was Rob's finest role, writing: 'The movie just seems lifeless and inert. Budget constraints leave the movie imprisoned largely at the estate grounds where Jugg is convalescing. While costumes may be accurate, I never felt transported to the 1940s. This came across more like a contemporary cast in a film using visual gimmickry – like blue-filtered shots which obscured events on screen, rapid edits, and unconvincing usage of stock footage for flashback sequences – to mask the fact that the script can't even sustain its comparatively brief running length.

The performances aren't bad per se but they are perfunctory. Pattinson, especially, seems a bit listless here. The scares seem staged and unconvincing, and the drama is resolved in a hokey and unsatisfying conclusion. All in all, *The Haunted Airman* is a slow-moving BBC production. I'm all about character-driven horror, and I wish there were more of it. However, this film has neither the script nor the staging to pull off the psychology effectively.'

Rob's next job was playing the quirky, oddball character of Daniel Gale in *The Bad Mother's Handbook* for ITV. This TV movie was based on the Kate Long novel of the same name and starred Catherine Tate, Anne Reid and Holliday Grainger. The plot centred on the lives of a grandmother, mother and daughter – with Rob's character dating the teenage daughter.

The movie is well worth watching as super-geek Daniel (Rob) is hilarious at times. He becomes friends with Charlie quite by accident after moving to her school. When she is dumped by her boyfriend she decides to kiss Daniel to try and make her ex jealous and agrees to go on a date with him. They strike up an unusual friendship and he is the one she turns to when she thinks she is pregnant, as she doesn't get on with her mum and her grandmother has dementia. Daniel and Charlie start to date, and although their personalities are very different they seem to work as a couple. Daniel supports her throughout her pregnancy and is there to hold her hand as she gives birth.

The Bad Mother's Handbook received a score of 6.6 out of

10 from IMDb, based on 1,149 reviews. *DVD Verdict*'s Roman Martel wrote in his review: 'Daniel [played by Rob] is an interesting character. He shows up at Charlotte's school as a transfer student, geeky and awkward. As the son of a doctor, he has a lot of medical knowledge, which he will spout out when the occasion warrants. He is obviously drawn to Charlotte, even if she thinks he's a big loser. But he's understanding and wants to help. Pattinson does a really good job of channeling compassion and confusion all at the same time. When he spouts out pregnancy symptoms while looking more and more uncomfortable it was pretty funny. He ends up providing much of the humor in the film.

'Since it was made for TV, you can expect a happy ending… and that's what we get. But there are some interesting twists along the way, especially when Karen battles with the decision to seek out her birth mother. All told, I found the characters interesting and the story, while a little standard, worth spending the time with.'

Rob's next project was so small that you will hardly find any information on it anywhere. *The Summer House* (2009) was an independent British movie in which Rob plays the part of Richard, a grovelling boyfriend who cheats on his girlfriend and then has to follow her to France to try and win her back. Just twelve minutes long, it had a really low budget. It was made for film festivals and there was no DVD release. It was the first part where Rob had to be sexy on screen, since his character has a passionate embrace with his on-off girlfriend Jane (played by Talulah Riley) during a party to celebrate the Moon landing.

The Summer House received a score of 5.9 out of 10 from IMDb, based on 495 reviews. Daniel Walber from *Spout* comments: 'Pattinson spends much of the film standing just off screen, hinted at but not introduced directly until the last few minutes (which probably helps his performance). He turns out to be quite the opposite of a gentle romantic paramour, perhaps an attempt to fight type-casting, though I'm not sure how effective that is.'

Although Rob enjoyed playing Toby in *The Haunted Airman*, Daniel in *The Bad Mother's Handbook* and Richard in *The Summer House*, by the time 2008 came round he was feeling a bit deflated. Being cast as Art in the comedy drama *How to Be* (2008), however, reignited his passion for acting. He divulged to *IFC*: 'I really felt that I didn't know whether I wanted to be an actor. I didn't know what I was doing, I hadn't gone to university...you know, I was kind of bumming around and not feeling very good at anything but at the same time desperately wanting to be, but thinking that you'll never reach your own... the goals you set yourself.'

How to Be was written and directed by the relatively unknown Oliver Irving. He wanted Rob to look as ugly as possible so got him to grow his hair long and have a strange hairstyle to play Art. He also gave him trousers that were too short and ill-fitting T-shirts and sweaters. Rob was asked to bring some of his own clothes to add to Art's wardrobe, so in the end about 50 per cent of Art's clothes were Rob's.

> **DID YOU KNOW?**
> After filming wrapped, Rob kept hold of some of Art's clothes to wear afterwards – which seems strange considering how awful they were.

Rob found playing Art really interesting and it made him want to keep on acting. When chatting to *IFC* about his character, he said: 'He's kind of, I guess you'd call him kind of a mediocrity – I mean, he doesn't really fit into any kind of people grouping. He's not particularly depressed, but he thinks he is. He doesn't have any kind of consistency in his emotions, which I think most people are like. Normally in films, if somebody's a sad person, they're a sad person but he's not particularly sad all the time – he's just basically chasing his tail. He's just a guy who is really stuck in a rut and he needs to figure a way out of it. I've never really felt stuck in anything. Art really feels like he's been trapped by his own life and he's kind of resentful about it as well. It would be really difficult to be friends with someone like Art. It seems like he's very real, but really he's a very demanding friend, he's very emotionally draining.'

Art is the movie's central character. He's an odd, quirky guy who is fed up of feeling miserable because he is stuck in a dead-end job and his girlfriend has dumped him. In an attempt to get his life back on track, he hires a self-help guru to come and live with him and his parents.

The movie premiered at the 2008 Slamdance Film Festival and was given the Grand Jury Honourable Mention for Narrative Feature award. It went on to be shown at almost twenty other film festivals during 2008/09. At the Strasbourg International Film Festival Rob won the Best Actor award and the movie picked up four more awards at various festivals.

> **DID YOU KNOW?**
> It was watching Rob as Art that inspired *Moviefone* to include him in their list of 'The Hottest Actors Under 25'.

How to Be was an independent, low-budget movie and a wide distribution wasn't on the cards until Rob's success in playing Edward Cullen in *Twilight* made thousands of his fans want to see the movie. Oliver Irving was able not only to release the movie on DVD but also to sell the soundtrack, which included Rob singing two tracks, 'Chokin' on the Dust' and 'Doin' Fine'.

How to Be received a score of 5.7 out of 10 from IMDb, based on 3,316 reviews. *Reel Film Reviews* thought the movie was terrible and only gave it 1 out of 4 stars. They said: 'Filmmaker Oliver Irving has infused *How To Be* with an oppressively deadpan vibe that cements its downfall right from the outset, as there's never a point at which the central character becomes a three-dimensional, fully fleshed-out figure worthy of the viewer's sympathy (i.e. despite Pattinson's best efforts, Arthur remains an aggressively synthetic figure from start to finish).

'And though billed as a comedy, *How to Be* suffers from a total absence of laughs that's made all-the-more noticeable by Irving's infuriatingly affected modus operandi (i.e. Napoleon Dynamite comes off as naturalistic and understated by comparison). It's a shame, really, as the film's subject matter could've been employed as a launching pad for an honest portrait of the central character's efforts at overcoming a quarter-life crisis; instead, *How to Be* ultimately boasts the feel of an ill-advised three-minute SNL sketch that's been ungainly expanded to feature length.'

Peter Debruge from *Variety* wrote in his review: 'An apathetic and uninteresting young Brit, played by Robert Pattinson (Cedric Diggory of the *Harry Potter* series), recruits a Canadian self-help guru to assist him with sorting out his relatively trivial personal issues in *How to Be*, a taxing reminder that middle-class depression ranks among cinema's least engaging topics. Winner of Slamdance's special jury honorable mention, this pic represents the other side of the "Control" coin, depicting the mopey adolescent despair of a wannabe rocker who lacks any sign of Ian Curtis's musical talent. Droll comedy could connect with UK youth, but seems doomed to homevid abroad.'

CHAPTER 6

ONWARDS AND UPWARDS

At the age of twenty-one Rob decided that he needed to leave London and move to America in order to take his acting career up to the next level. His agent Stephanie Ritz had absolute faith in him and offered to put him up in her Malibu home because she knew he would make something of himself if he just got a lucky break.

Despite having lived in his own place in London Rob wasn't very domesticated. He wasn't very good at cleaning his clothes and couldn't cook even the most basic of meals. Really, he needed someone to mother him. He drank far too much Diet Coke and became addicted to Cinnamon Toast Crunch cereal.

Rob and Stephanie decided that he should audition for a romantic comedy called *Post Grad*, which was being directed by Vicky Jenson (who would go on to direct *Shrek* in 2001 and

Shark Tale in 2004). Rob was convinced he could win the part of Adam Davies, the main character's love interest, but alas it wasn't to be.

'I was so into the script of it and thought I knew exactly what I was doing,' he told *The Hollywood Reporter*. 'And then I went in and just completely blew it. And honestly, I remember talking to my family afterwards and going, "I'm done. I can't handle how gut-wrenching it is." And I kind of knew that I was messing it up. It was my own fault.'

Thankfully Rob's family and Stephanie managed to convince him to stick it out and go to other auditions. When he got the call to say he would be playing the legendary Salvador Dalí in the Paul Morrison directed movie *Little Ashes* he was stoked.

It was a movie he had first auditioned for two years previously but that didn't dampen his enthusiasm, as he had one of the main parts. Initially, he had been cast as Federico García Lorca but a year later, he had been asked to read for the part of Salvador Dalí instead. Things went quiet on the project, but then Rob was contacted by the movie's producers out of the blue to say that they finally had the funding they needed. Rob didn't have much time to gather his thoughts as filming was starting in Barcelona, Spain, just four days later. Thankfully, he didn't have any other projects lined up so could fly out and join his fellow actors.

Little Ashes is a Spanish-English drama set in the 1920s and 1930s, and tells the story of three of the most creative talents of that era: Luis Buñuel, Salvador Dalí and Federico García Lorca. Rob did so well taking on the challenge of playing Salvador Dalí because he couldn't speak any Spanish.

Rob might have kept a character diary to play Cedric Diggory in *Harry Potter and the Goblet of Fire* but he knew he had to up his game for *Little Ashes* and writing a diary alone wouldn't be enough. Because he was playing a real person for the first time, he felt a greater responsibility to make sure that he portrayed Salvador Dalí correctly. This time he had to try to become the Spanish surrealist. Rob explained to *MoviesOnline*: 'I had this whole series of photos and I figured out the way he would move his body. There's a picture of him pointing. I spent days trying to figure it out, "How did he get his arm like that?"

'It was the first time that I had ever got into characterisation, trying to work on movements. I was doing tons of stuff on his walk and such. It was probably unnecessary, but it was the one time I felt, like, slightly satisfied. But I wanted to bring that intensity to every job.'

One of the most challenging parts of the movie for Rob were the nude scenes, as he found them embarrassing. He confessed to *Star* magazine: 'It's funny because Spanish people have no problem with nudity at all, and I mean at all. And English people obviously do have the most enormous problem with it. Little things, like when I saw my father getting changed for swimming, I was traumatised by it...I kind of freaked out a bit.'

He explained more in an interview with *GQ* magazine after the movie was released: 'I thought I'd never get another acting job again…so I was like, "Yeah – why not try to do something weird?" There's all these gay-sex scenes. And, you know, I haven't even done a sex scene with a girl in my whole career.

'Here I am, with Javier [Beltrán], who plays [Federico García] Lorca, doing an extremely hard-core sex scene, where I have a nervous breakdown afterward … And because we're both straight, what we were doing seemed kind of ridiculous. … And it wasn't even a closed set. There were all these Spanish electricians giggling to themselves.'

The movie had a budget of €2,500,000 and was first screened at the 2008 Raindance Film Festival in London on 7 October 2008. It was also screened at Spain's Valladolid Film Festival just three weeks later on 27 October 2008. *Little Ashes* was not intended to be a mainstream movie but Rob's success in *Twilight* resulted in a worldwide DVD release in 2009.

Rob was very pleased that he was able to give the movie a boost, telling journalist Laremy Legel at the time: 'I did two little movies last year [*How to Be* and *Little Ashes*]. Without *Twilight*, I don't know what would happen to them. They would get like one theatre, tiny. I love it when people come up to me and say, "I'm not actually a fan of yours from *Twilight*, I'm a fan of yours from the poster of *Little Ashes*." It's so funny.'

Little Ashes received a score of 6.6 out of 10 from IMDb, based on 6,774 reviews.

Claudia Puig from *USA Today* gave the movie 2 out of 4 stars, writing: 'The dialogue is stilted in an attempt to be profound. Most of the actors speak English with Spanish accents, except Pattinson, who employs a pretentious kooky-speak, accompanied by wild-eyed expressions. When he's emotional, he throws dark paint on a canvas and all over himself. Rage, frustration, sadness? It's anybody's guess.

'A long-delayed kiss between Dalí and Lorca while swimming in a moonlit sea is beautifully photographed. While the visuals are stunning and the guitar-infused score evocative, they don't make up for the silly script.

'Pattinson spouts such narcissistic baubles as: "Time and Dalí wait for no man" and "Spain just seems so passé." Such pap can't hope to pierce the mystique of one of the 20th century's most influential artists. *Little Ashes* instead piques our interest in Lorca.'

Digital Spy's review was slightly more complimentary and gave the movie 3 out of 5 stars: 'In making a film about three revolutionary artists in their formative years, Morrison has immense scope to delve into their genius and find out what made them tick. To *Little Ashes*'s detriment, he never peels back those layers and investigates what stirred their minds, instead focusing on what stirred their loins. It does succeed, however, in capturing a decadent, bohemian spirit pulsing through a country on the verge of massive social reform.

'Pattinson has to work hard to overcome his teen idol tag,

but acquits himself well with a solid Spanish accent and dials into just about the right level of googly-eyed weirdness to keep his Dalí credible. It's only elements out of his control that let him down, such as a selection of bad wigs and the comic reveal of him wearing the famous tweaked moustache. And goodness knows what Twilighters will think of the scene where he masturbates while watching Lorca have sex! It might be frolicky and slightly frivolous, but *Little Ashes*'s Entourageian take on the lives of Spain's artistic elite has a fiery passion and some fine central performances.'

CHAPTER 7

TAKING A CHANCE

When the opportunity arose to audition for the lead male part in a new teen book adaption called *Twilight*, Rob wasn't sure if it was even worth wasting his time. Edward Cullen was supposed to be the 'most handsome man on the planet' and he felt anything but. In some ways he felt that just by auditioning he was humiliating himself because he simply wasn't good-looking enough to stand a chance. In the end, he decided to give it a go, and boy, is he glad he did!

He sent the director, Catherine Hardwicke, an audition tape that he'd filmed in London, 'with Tom [Sturridge] playing Bella.' A while later, she rang him to invite him to audition in person for the role, but because of the time difference it was 2.30 in the morning. Rob recalled to *The Hollywood Reporter*: '[We had] this ridiculous conversation, and I hadn't read the books or the script or anything and I just bullshitted on the phone.'

Despite making it to the next stage Rob still wasn't convinced he was good-looking enough to play Edward. 'The Edward in the book is like an enigma of everything that's perfect about a man,' he confided in the *Irish Central*, 'It's like, "He walked into a room and it hurts to see how beautiful he is". It's just kind of embarrassing. I just couldn't figure out a way to act perfect, I felt like an idiot going into the audition.'

Rob knew little about *Twilight* when he made his audition tape but he wanted to try something new after stretching himself in *Little Ashes*. He divulged to journalist Rebecca Murray: 'I didn't want to do a stupid teen movie. I specifically hadn't done anything which anyone would see since *Harry Potter* because I wanted to teach myself how to act. I didn't want to be an idiot. This came kind of randomly and I didn't really know what it was when it first started. I was going to wait for another year. I wanted to do two or three more little things and then do something bigger. And then this kind of happened and I was like, "Well, okay…"'

Playing Salvador Dalí had been so satisfying for Rob that he was actually on a bit of a high when he auditioned for Edward. He revealed to *Collider.com*: 'I wanted to take that [satisfaction] into *Twilight* and also try to break down the assumption that if a movie is being made from a book which is selling a lot of copies – which every single book that sells a lot of copies now is made into a movie immediately and they're virtually all not very good and everyone knows, even six-year-olds know, that it's just to make money – I didn't want to be involved in something like that.'

Twilight director Catherine Hardwicke had seen hundreds of pretty boys wanting to play Edward but very few had given her goosebumps. Many had been good-looking but somehow didn't look right; they didn't look like the Edward she pictured in her head. She needed someone pale-skinned, who could really act.

When Rob stepped through her audition doors he actually felt quite relaxed. He wasn't worried about auditioning in front of Catherine, but later, when it came to doing his read-through with Kristen Stewart, he was nervous. Kristen had already been cast as Bella, the female lead, and she was much more confident about how she wanted to play the scene. 'I think she'd done about ten readings that day,' Rob told *Syfy. com*, 'I was kind of intimidated by what she was doing; I was stunned because it was so different from what I was expecting. And I guess it never really changed the whole way through, which kind of works, just in terms of the story, me having to be the powerful one but being intimidated by her. The relationship [was] built from that... We really weren't trying to act like we were in love with each other right from the beginning – it was more about trying to intimidate each other and showing how much we didn't care about the other person, which I guess worked. In a lot of ways, that's how long-lasting relationships work.'

Catherine was impressed with Rob's audition with Kristen but she wanted to see if they had chemistry. She invited him and three other actors to her house for a final audition. He had to prove to her that he was the right actor to play Edward by kissing Kristen on her bed. Kristen kissed the three other guys first and then it was Rob's turn. In many ways it was the most important kiss of his life!

Rob put everything into the kiss, he didn't hold back because he wanted the part so badly. It went so well that Catherine had to tell them to tone it down because they were so passionate. Rob revealed to the *Daily Record*: 'It was funny. When I got into bed with Kristen I said, "I've only known you for an hour and we are in bed." I think I must have gone way over the top with it as well, because I remember looking up afterwards and Catherine Hardwicke had a look on her face as if to say, "What are you doing? You look like you're having a seizure!"'

> **DID YOU KNOW?**
> Rob refused to take his top off during the audition. He told *The Hollywood Reporter*, 'They were doing screen tests with four people. In one of the scenes, I [was meant] to take my shirt off, and I think I was the one guy who didn't.'

Afterwards, Kristen told Catherine that Rob had to get the part – he had been so much better than the other actors who had been shortlisted. She explained to a journalist from the *Philippine Daily Enquirer* why he had been her favourite: 'Rob came into the audition looking sort of terrified, like a subdued fear and pained; the pain was just very evident in him. I am not saying it's in Rob, but he knew what to bring to that character. We didn't need the statuesque, model-types who come in and just pose. I couldn't see any of the other guys – they weren't even looking at me, it was like they were focusing on their lines – but Rob is very organic. He's in the moment and he lets it happen, which is brave. He's brave. He's a courageous actor.'

DID YOU KNOW?
Some of the producers at Lionsgate had initially thought that Rob was too old to play Edward because he was twenty-one but once they met him they changed their minds. Rob revealed to *The Hollywood Reporter*: 'Stephanie [Ritz, his agent] was like, "You've got to go and meet the producers and just shave 20 times before you go."'

Catherine didn't really need Kristen to tell her that Rob was the right person to play Edward, she already knew the part belonged to him. However, she did have to convince the bosses at Summit Film Studio and Lionsgate that he was right for the role. Rob was relatively unknown, his hair was still dyed black from playing Salvador Dalí in *Little Ashes* and he was heavier than they envisaged Edward to be, but Catherine knew he had lots of potential. She knew that with a bit of work, he could be 'the most handsome man on the planet'. Thankfully, they backed her and Rob 100 per cent.

The movie's screenwriter Melissa Rosenberg didn't have a hand to play in choosing Rob to play Edward as casting was not in her remit but she was filled with excitement when she met him and Kristen for the first time. Meeting them actually made her think about Edward and Bella in a different light. She told *Hit Fix*: 'When I first saw them, when they were first brought on, I was just stunned at how perfect the casting was. And Catherine [Hardwicke] did a really extraordinary job of finding them. And interestingly when I wrote *Twilight*, before they came on, I [tended to] lean toward humour and sometimes broad humour, sometimes very dark humour so I added a lot of that into the *Twilight* script. It wasn't right. So I actually kind of went a little bit away from the book, I think, in some ways and the actors brought me and the screenplay back into actually more of the tone of the book.'

Stephenie Meyer, author of the *Twilight Saga*, had originally wanted Henry Cavill, of *Stardust* and *Tudors* fame, to play Edward but he was too old at twenty-four so couldn't even be considered. After Catherine introduced her to Rob and she saw how well he could act, she gave him her full backing. She knew he would make a great Edward.

Having the support of Catherine, Melissa and Stephenie must have given Rob a huge boost. He was slated by many fans of the books as soon as his casting was announced, with over 75,000 people signing a petition to get the role re-cast, but once Stephenie gave him her backing, the hate campaign lost steam. Fans became much more open to him and wanted to see what he was like in the movie before judging him – all because they trusted Stephenie's opinion.

This must have been a relief for not just Rob but his family too. Rob confessed to *The Big Issue*: 'People sent me hate mail and the Internet was full of messages from *Twilight* fans who didn't want me. They said I looked like a bum. My mother told me she had read online that I was wretched and ugly, and had the face of a gargoyle.'

DID YOU KNOW?

Stephenie Meyer claims she knew Rob would become famous right from the very beginning. She admitted to *Entertainment Weekly* shortly after he was cast: 'I apologised to Rob for ruining his life. There is going to be a group of girls who will follow his actions from now on. I asked the producer, "Is Rob ready for this? Have you guys prepped him? Is he ready to be the 'It Guy?'" I don't think he really is – I don't think he sees himself that way. And I think the transition is going to be a little rocky.'

CHAPTER 8

BECOMING EDWARD

*T*wilight was to be filmed in Portland, Oregon, and the surrounding area. Portland was chosen as the location because its often-cloudy skies fitted with the fictional town, Forks, where the story is set. The town's weather could change from sunny to stormy in an instant.

Rob had a free schedule so decided to travel to Portland months before filming was due to start so that he could get a feel for the place and focus on how he wanted to play Edward. He knew that he had a lot of preparation to do and being in Portland on his own meant that he wouldn't be distracted.

He was able to draw on the experience he had gained from developing his characters in *How To Be*, *The Bad Mother's Handbook*, *Little Ashes* and all the other projects he had done since *Harry Potter and the Goblet of Fire*. He wanted

Twilight to show him at his best. He might not have been to drama school but he had learnt so much from playing different characters.

Rob chatted to French magazine *15 à 20* about how he went about preparing to play Edward. He said: 'I don't know how it started [laughs] but I hadn't realised how difficult it was going to be to play Edward until I started reading the script. He's a very complex character. So I moved to Portland on my own, two or three months before filming began, and I didn't do anything but read the script and books to find anything that helped me play him. So I started to write things. I mean, if you really prepare for a role, there's going to be a moment in which he's all you can think of. So, I did things like little suicide notes. I was a little worrying, actually [bursts out laughing].'

In a separate interview with *Tu* magazine he revealed how spending time on his own made him wary of speaking to other people. He said: 'If you don't speak to another person in a few weeks, you start feeling afraid of them, even when you order food at a restaurant. If I didn't go to pubs or bars, I would be running away in the middle of the night [laughs].'

As part of his preparation he spent time with the *Twilight Sagas'* author Stephenie Meyer, getting her opinion on things. From speaking to Stephenie he was able to get a clearer picture of the Edward she had created and was able to understand him more. He didn't just have to draw inspiration from the *Twilight*,

New Moon, *Eclipse* and *Breaking Dawn* books, as Stephenie very kindly shared *Midnight Sun* with him.

Midnight Sun was *Twilight*, but written from Edward's perspective. It was top-secret, Stephenie hadn't shared it with many people as it needed a lot of work doing to it. It was just a rough draft but Stephenie felt that it could help Rob understand how Edward struggles to control his urge to kill. She also shared it with *Twilight*'s director Catherine Hardwicke so she would understand too.

'In the book [*Twilight*] it seems that when he says, "I'm a monster and I'm going to kill you," and she says, "I'm not afraid," you kind of know the whole time in the book that he's never going to do anything bad. But then you read that first chapter in *Midnight Sun* where the full extent of how much he wanted to kill her and how he's considering killing the entire school just so that he can kill her becomes evident,' Rob explained to *About.com*. 'I wanted that element of him to be very prominent. I wanted Bella to be saying, "I'm not scared. You won't do anything to me?" but not so certainly so that it'd suddenly be like, "You won't do anything to me, will you?" I kind of wanted something like that. I think it makes it sexier if there's a very real chance of him just flipping out and killing her.'

Rob kept his copy of *Midnight Sun* safe and didn't share it with anyone else but somehow the book was leaked on 28 August 2008. To say that Stephenie was upset when she found out would be an understatement, she was devastated.

On her official website, she posted: 'So where does this leave *Midnight Sun*? My first feeling was that there was no way to continue. Writing isn't like math; in math, two plus two always equals four, no matter what your mood is like. With writing, the way you feel changes everything. If I tried to write *Midnight Sun* now, in my current frame of mind, James would probably win and all the Cullens would die, which wouldn't dovetail too well with the original story. In any case, I feel too sad about what has happened to continue working on *Midnight Sun*, and so it is on hold indefinitely.'

Stephenie decided to allow fans of her books to download a draft of *Midnight Sun* directly from her website because she didn't want them downloading the stolen version.

> **DID YOU KNOW?**
> At the time Stephenie thought that someone had hacked into her emails to steal *Midnight Sun* but she later realised that an earlier draft she had asked for feedback on must have been photocopied.

Stephenie might have created Edward Cullen but in Rob's eyes that didn't mean that she was 100 per cent right about the way he should play him. He enjoyed debating with her about why the Edward in the movie needed to be different from the one in her books. They spent hours discussing the matter but in the end, they just had to agree to disagree.

He told *goodprattle.com*: 'I was talking to Stephenie Meyer, saying, "The guy must be chronically depressed," and she was saying, "No, he's not, he's not, he's not." But I still maintain he was. I mean, it's not like depressed, but just this sort of loneliness. I mean, when you see him at school, he doesn't really talk to anyone. He must get bored after a while only hanging out with the same four people in his life.'

Some members of the press wrongly reported that Rob and Stephenie had had a huge argument and had fallen out because of their opposing views. This simply wasn't true. Stephenie set the record straight in an interview for ReelzChannel. She said: 'It wasn't an argument, but we [did] actually disagree on his character. I'd be like, "No, this is how it is." He's like, "No, it's definitely this way." Yet in the performance he did what he wanted, and yet it was exactly what I wanted.'

Rob found playing Edward and understanding his mentality a huge challenge. He spent a long time thinking about whether Edward would have the mentality of a one-hundred-and-eight-year-old or a seventeen-year-old, as he had been seventeen when Carlisle turned him into a vampire, back in 1918. His character had been dying of the Spanish influenza in Chicago when Carlisle took the decision to 'save' his life by turning him into a vampire.

Then Rob shared with MTV how he believed that it would have been kinder for Carlisle to have let Edward die instead of turning him into a vampire. He said: 'The way a vampire gets made is you just get bitten by someone. I mean, it's just like a disease. They're not separate entities to the rest of the world, they are much more human. You're just a human, you get bitten by another human who's been turned into this thing, and you just have to live forever afterwards. And you have these powers, you have super-strength and really amazing agility, but the pros for being a vampire don't really outweigh the cons at all. You can never reveal that you're a vampire, so you're just trapped in this kind of purgatory all the time. You can do a couple of cool things [laughs]. But it gets old after, like, 400 years. And also, you have to go around killing people all the time, which is another bummer.'

Conversations like this show how much of a deep thinker Rob is at times and how he sometimes tries to think logically about something that is illogical. [If Edward hadn't been turned into a vampire there would have been no *Twilight* at the end of the day.]

Rob couldn't understand why girls find vampires like Edward so appealing but Kristen Stewart knew why: 'It's because vampires are classically meant to draw you into the point where they have you in a complete submitting state to where they can kill you. So that's a little bit sexy, to completely let something take over. It's forbidden fruit. It's something you can't have, you just want more,' she told *Movies Online*.

Often the research Rob did brought up more questions than answers. Had another actor been cast as Edward it is very unlikely that they would have dedicated even half as much time to researching and developing the character as Rob did. Maybe they would have looked at *Twilight* as just a low-budget teen movie and tried to get by with as little preparation as possible, but this is not something that would have sat right with Rob. He is an extremely conscientious person and needed to understand as much as he could about Edward in order to play him convincingly.

He explained to *Vanity Fair*: 'When his life is put into basic terms, he has nothing to live for and all he wants to do is either become a human or die. The only reason that he hasn't died is because he is too scared; he doesn't think that he has a soul. Then he meets Bella, who makes him feel like a human and feel alive again. At the same time, her human vulnerability makes him incredibly vulnerable, because even with his super speed and his super strength, he still can't fully protect her. Whenever she is in danger, he is in danger. If she dies or goes anywhere, then he is gone, too.'

Rob might have enjoyed the process of getting under the skin of Edward's character but getting physically ready to play him wasn't anywhere near as enjoyable. He was to play the most handsome man/vampire on the planet and the movie's producers thought his teeth were letting him down. In order to give him a Hollywood smile, they suggested he had an operation on his gums to 'correct' his teeth.

In fact Rob has never been a vain person, not even when he

was a model, so the idea of having an operation to fix his teeth seemed ridiculous to him. He confessed to a reporter from *B96*: 'Yeah, they tried to put a brace on me. I'll hold that against the people who decided that. The amount of stuff they wanted to do to my teeth – they wanted to give me gum surgery and put this like, Invisalign thing [special plastic liners that are used to move teeth, like braces do] on and I was just [shocked face] and the producers were like, "How much is that going to cost?" and I was just listening, going "Wwwwwwait, I'm not cutting all my gums off! What are you talking about?"

'I didn't, I just pretended. They did the whole Invisalign thing, the whole treatment. I wore it for maybe fifteen minutes and then I told the producers I was wearing it for a good month-and-a-half before I had the guts to tell them. People were saying, "Your teeth look so much better" – it's the power of suggestion.'

He was also told he needed to get fitter, so started to work out to lose some of the weight he had put on while filming *Little Ashes*. Rob exercised so much that it made Catherine Hardwicke worried about his health. 'I used to go to the gym for about five hours a day but then I started losing so such weight. My head started to look really huge in comparison to the rest of my body. [Director Catherine Hardwicke] came up to me and said, "What are you doing to yourself?" To gain weight, I literally stopped exercising. Eating a cheeseburger after two-and-a-half months of doing that – it tasted like ambrosia,' Rob confessed to *Entertainment Weekly*.

And he had to learn to drive, which was a challenge-and-a-half, but he somehow managed to pass after a ten-hour crash course and was awarded an International Licence. He felt confident enough to drive on set but driving on real roads was another thing completely. At first he felt okay driving around on his own but once the paparazzi started recognising him, he lost his nerve. They drove too close to him and made him feel under pressure.

Once it was time to start filming Rob had to go through the ordeal of transforming himself into Edward each day. Getting his make-up applied took hours because he had to be so pale and he had to wear coloured contact lenses that really irritated his eyes. Simply putting in his lenses took him forty minutes each day so he had to arrive on set hours before the cameras started rolling so he could get ready.

Having to put on an American accent to play Edward wasn't a challenge for Rob, even though he had never had any form of accent training. He had simply picked it up from watching American movies and TV shows. He made a conscious decision to keep speaking with an American accent even when the cameras stopped rolling, explaining to MTV: 'For the big dialogue scenes, it's just easier to not keep switching between. I kind of do it by accident. I keep forgetting that I'm speaking in an American accent sometimes. The dangerous thing is that you end up forgetting what your real accent is after a while!'

Rob might be confident speaking with an American accent

but he doesn't feel his other accents are very convincing, telling one reporter: 'American's fine, but I've never really been a big one for accents. Whenever I try to do any accents, it ends up being a sort of Jamaican-Russian hybrid.'

Kristen Stewart might have only been seventeen when she met Rob for the first time but she seemed much older. She had appeared in fifteen movies, including *Jumper* with Samuel L. Jackson (2008) and *Panic Room* with Jodie Foster in 2002, meaning that she was one of the most experienced members of the *Twilight* cast. Kristen was completely dedicated to being the best actress she could be and wasn't going to be dominated by anyone. She was fiercely passionate about playing Bella and appreciated how much Catherine Hardwicke let her shape her character.

From his initial audition with Kristen, Rob picked up how strong she was, telling *goodprattle.com*: 'She's not the kind of damsel in distress at all.' He felt inferior to her in the beginning because she had been in so many more movies than he had. He spilled the beans to *Entertainment Weekly*: 'In the beginning I thought to myself, "Because she's so serious, I've got to be really serious." I didn't speak for about two months so I would seem really intense – I would only ever talk about the movie. And I kept recommending all these books. It didn't work, though. Then I started falling apart and my character started breaking down. I felt like an idiot, just following her around, saying, "You really should read some Zola – and there's this amazing

Truffaut movie." And she started calling me on things: "Have you actually watched this movie? Yeah? What's it about?" "It's about a guy on a train." "Did you just look at the photo on the corner of the DVD?"'

As they got to know each other more he realised that they both shared the character trait of not being able to back down to people. Kristen became someone he could turn to if he had a problem during filming and they discussed their scenes at great lengths before shooting them. They both felt that the kissing scenes were the key relationship ones as well – and that Edward and Bella couldn't kiss like normal people. Rob explained to MTV: 'The whole thing about both of them is that they think they should be able to, but there's always the elephant in the room. I always want to kill her, like all the time.'

Their attention to even the slightest detail shows how dedicated they were to making sure that *Twilight* and the later movies were the best they could be. Neither of them wanted to make 'just another teen movie'.

On their first day of filming Rob managed to injure himself but thankfully he didn't do himself any lasting damage. He was filming the climax to the movie, the ballet studio scene. He confessed to *MoviesOnline*: 'I went to pick up Krist and I almost ripped my hamstring. It's not even a stunt. She weighs like, 50 pounds – I literally did one squat. And this was after three months of training.'

He also filmed the baseball scene that day, which was tricky to shoot because he had never played baseball and his hand-to-eye coordination isn't the best. Edward was supposed to be a great player so Catherine had to get someone to teach Rob how to play – and fast.

'I'm terrible – I'm completely mal-coordinated, I'm terrible at all sports. Also, I don't see the point as well. I even had a baseball coach. Catherine was so determined to make me look like a professional baseball player and I literally couldn't take it seriously,' he told *MoviesOnline*.

Catherine was always honest with Rob and wasn't afraid to tell him when he was doing things wrong. In turn, he really admired her directing skills and the way she treated the cast and crew. He shared with the *Los Angeles Times*: 'She's such a free spirit! She has no filter – she kind of gets you out of nowhere. Like she'd go, "You know that thing you're doing there? Yeah, that. That's not good." And I'd go, "Really?" And she'd say, "Yeah, it's weird. And it's not working. At all." The diplomacy department is not her finest. But you love that about her, that she feels free to say, "That sucked. Try something subtler," which is really her way of saying *you* sucked.'

Filming *Twilight* was really enjoyable for him and he has many fond memories that he will treasure forever. He told *Vanity Fair*: 'I knew that there were some scenes where I was going to have to look demonic and have a glare that would scare humans. That was difficult to prepare. My favourite scene that we ended up shooting was this little random one near the beginning where I try and intimidate Bella by being a scary vampire and she doesn't back down at all.'

But he didn't enjoy filming the treetop scenes because of the pain his harness caused him. He told the *Twilight Lexicon*: 'Because you're balancing your entire weight on two straps, like in your crotch, and also being pulled at 35 mph and pretending to run, which makes it chafe against everything, it was just really, really unpleasant. And to make it real, you really have to go into the most painful position. Like, if you try to do anything to ease the pain, it makes it look really fake, so it wasn't really fun.'

As filming continued Rob picked up a few more little injuries but it was Kristen's stunt double who really suffered for the movie. Rob accidentally dropped her while they filmed the car-stop scene, leaving her struggling to walk for a few weeks. He explained what happened to *MyParkMag*: 'The scariest stunt was when I run and I put my hand out to stop this car which is racing towards me. I had practised it a bunch of times but the car is like, coming at 30 miles per hour. And I was sick on the day of shooting. I had taken antibiotics and I was really dozy, and the car went off its tracks. So there I am, holding Kristen's stunt double and my timing was off because I wasn't feeling too good and the car like, hit me in the face. Then I dropped her and I couldn't stop laughing.'

Rob had to leave some of his more dangerous stunts to his own stunt double, Paul Darnell, as Catherine couldn't afford for him to injury himself, since it would hold up filming. He explained to journalist Sheila Roberts: 'I can do something, and get injured and look like crap playing it, or he can do it and make it look really good, and no one notices the difference. After a while, I tried to do the Tom Cruise thing, but I eventually gave up.'

DID YOU KNOW?
Rob thanked Paul in his acceptance speech at the 2009 MTV Movie Awards when he won the Best Fight award with Cam Gigandet (who played James).

Catherine told MTV while they were shooting: 'I do feel lucky directing Kristen and Rob, because their faces are so beautiful. They're expressive. Their skin is just porcelain, and sometimes I am literally watching the monitor and I'm going, "Oh, I'm so excited!" just jumping up and down. But I don't say anything, because I want to keep them in the moment. Sometimes I feel like I'm getting gold here. And it is very exciting.'

Stephenie Meyer felt exactly the same, telling the *Los Angeles Times*: 'The thing is, he looks different when he does characters. When you watch the films that he's done, you might not be able to put [them] together with the same person because he's such a chameleon. There were times when he was just being Rob and then you'd hear "Action!" and he'd step into character – and he'd look different! He'd sound like Edward! It was crazy. He did such a good job.'

> **DID YOU KNOW?**
> Rob was ordered to stay out of the sun and not get a tan because he needed to be as pale as possible to play Edward. He told *You* magazine: 'I don't like being in the sun anyway, which is pretty lucky. I'm English so I don't go there. I just go [laughter] red. I don't even go tanned. I guess you could have a red vampire, which makes a little bit of sense.'

The filming schedule for the movie was tight so all the cast and crew were under pressure to try and get things right first time. This meant that the unpredictable weather became a real problem – as sudden downpours ruined shots and resulted in filming having to stop for several hours at a time.

Even the highly experienced Catherine Hardwicke found it tough. She struggled so much when the weather was terrible that she was reduced to tears on more than one occasion. She pulled herself together when she saw the dedication of local fans who stood watching them film even in the pouring rain and hail. They weren't going to let rain dampen their enthusiasm for *Twilight*.

Rob found the way the weather changed at a moment's notice very strange, telling *Hollywood.com*: 'Oregon has the strangest weather stuff that happens, especially in the spring when we were shooting. It would be like, sunny, snowing, raining and hailing at exactly the same time. Though it could be raining, there'd be no clouds in the sky and stuff. I don't know, it was like fake weather.'

For Catherine Hardwicke to choose a leading lady who was just seventeen was risky because Kristen could only legally work for a maximum of five hours a day. Bella appears in pretty much every scene in *Twilight* so the whole cast and crew had to make sure they were ready for action as soon as the cameras started rolling – they couldn't afford to have to keep retaking scenes. Rob and the rest of the cast were so pleased when Kristen turned eighteen on 9 April 2008 that they presented her with a birthday cake with 'Now you're on nights' written in icing on the top.

Having Kristen to talk to when *Twilight* was being filmed really helped Rob come out of his shell. Initially, some members of the crew had been concerned that he had spent so long getting under Edward's skin that it might have left him feeling down and miserable. In an attempt to cheer him up they followed him around the set and gave him a copy of *Twilight* in which they had highlighted all the passages in the book where Edward smiled or was happy. They felt this would help lift his mood, but in reality, Rob was just being Rob. It always seems to take him a while to warm up to people and feel relaxed in their company.

Rather than being concerned, Kristen found it quite funny that Rob got so involved in playing Edward that he kind of became Edward all the time, even when the cameras stopped rolling. She told *ET*: 'I had this little thing: "Rob, let's just rehearse the scene all the way through without tearing it down and criticising it." We'd get two lines out, and then he would say, "No, no, no, it's not working!" Rob made himself crazy the whole movie, and I just stopped and patted him on the back through his neuroses. He would punch me in the face if he heard me right now.'

CHAPTER 9

WORLD-FAMOUS

Summit Entertainment had planned to release *Twilight* to the world in December 2008 but they brought the release forward a month when the November release of *Harry Potter and the Half-Blood Prince* was postponed until the following July.

Despite not having to compete with *Harry Potter and the Half-Blood Prince*, *Twilight* was still going up against the Disney animated movie *Bolt*, which was also released the same day. Daniel Craig's *Quantum of Solace* had been released to much fanfare the weekend before and was still bringing in huge audiences. No one could predict what would happen. Would fans of the books make *Twilight* a success? Would it attract a whole new audience or would it be a flop?

When the cast arrived at the Los Angeles *Twilight* premiere they had a hint of what was to come. So many fans of the books turned up to see the actors and actresses playing their favourite characters. Rob really struggled to cope with the thousands upon thousands of fans screaming his name. The world's press were there too, with a seemingly endless number of photographers and reporters competing to get his attention. He felt under so much pressure that it was hard for him to smile. Indeed, he was so shaken up that ten minutes into the screening, he was forced to leave and had a panic attack in his car.

He found all the fans screaming at once overwhelming, telling the *Los Angeles Times* in a later interview: 'When you're greeted by crowds of screaming fans, it's like being in some medieval battle. I guess that's the closest analogy, especially after yesterday. A ton of people ran down the street outside the Apple Store. I felt like I was literally being charged by Celts.'

Against all odds, *Twilight* well and truly trounced the competition from day one of its release. On the opening day, *Twilight* took an amazing $35.7 million at the box office – almost covering the whole costs involved with making the film. It was the fourteenth-biggest first day ever for a film and made Catherine Hardwicke the first female director to have generated such a large sum on a first day, too.

As more and more people went to see *Twilight* and reported back to their friends how good it was, the numbers going to see the film kept growing and growing. By the end of the first week, everyone involved in *Twilight* and movies in general was flabbergasted by its success. *Twilight* received a score of 5.2 out of 10 from IMDb, based on 308,214 reviews.

Movie critics, however, were not impressed with the film and many wrote negative reviews. They felt that *Twilight* was underwhelming and thought that Rob had struggled to pull off the role of Edward, which was the complete opposite to how millions of cinemagoers felt when they saw the movie. It captured the hearts of millions of people – not just young girls. They flocked to the cinemas and left feeling it was the best film they'd ever seen. Quite a few had also been introduced to the man of their dreams for the first time.

Twilight's new, passionate fan base hit back at the negative reviews, criticising magazines such as *Empire*, who had said: 'Pattinson struggles at times – it's a demanding first lead role, requiring him to project a perennial restrained desire. He settles down eventually, but not before he's treated us to a series of hard-faced pouts.'

They backed magazines which gave positive reviews and felt that the US magazine *Entertainment Weekly* captured exactly how they were feeling. In their review they wrote: 'Edward is Romeo, Heathcliff, James Dean and Brad Pitt all rolled into one…a scruffy, gorgeous bloodsucker pin-up who is really an angelic protector.'

DID YOU KNOW?
If he hadn't been cast as Edward the only other role Rob would have liked to have played would have been James.

Many fans might have credited Rob and Stephenie Meyer with making *Twilight* a hit, but without Catherine Hardwicke and her passion a totally different movie would have been made, which would have left fans of the book reeling.

When Catherine had been given the first script she had been appalled – it had been worked on so much that it hardly resembled the story in Stephenie's book. She explained to *Time* magazine: 'Bella was a track star. Then there were FBI agents – the vampires would migrate south into Mexico every year, and FBI agents in Utah were tracking them. They ended up on an island, chasing everyone around on jet skis.'

Catherine had taken time out to read all of the *Twilight Saga* books and had fallen in love with the story. She contacted the talented screenwriter Melissa Rosenberg, and together they set about writing a new *Twilight* script from scratch. What they created together was pure magic, much to Rob's delight when he was handed a copy.

Some *Twilight* fans presumed that Rob was exactly like Edward (apart from him not being a vampire, obviously) but he insisted time and time again in his *Twilight* interviews that he was very different from his character. He reiterated to *Twist* magazine: 'Edward's this 108-year-old adult trapped inside a seventeen-year-old body, but I'm still a six-year-old boy at heart... I look a bit like him.'

DID YOU KNOW?

Rob had actually tried to read *Twilight* five months before his audition after someone recommended the book to him but he had given up after a few pages in because he thought it was too girly. Months later, on reading Catherine and Melissa's script he was impressed with the changes that had been made. He told the *Examiner*: 'It cut out a lot of the descriptions...It read more like an action script. So later, I went back to the book and saw what the differences had been. I looked at it a bit more objectively. I liked the book better when I came back to it the second time.'

He found it strange that so many teenage girls found Edward so irresistible. He told *Dose.ca*: 'If Edward was not a fictional character and you just met him in reality, you know, he's one of those guys who'd be like an axe murderer. He's ultra-polite and really formal all the time and like, "Let me open the door! Let me carry the bags!" Literally, you can just tell he'd freak out one day and shoot someone.'

Despite gaining millions of female fans the second *Twilight* was released Rob remained single. In November 2008, he told the *National Enquirer*: 'I'm not dating anyone. I mean, I theoretically don't avoid it, but it's weird. I've been going to the same places every time I go to LA because they're the only places I know. And now everybody kind of knows me in those places. So, it's like I don't know. Just knowing that people will talk about stuff, and – you know. It's very uncomfortable. And also, if you try and chat people up, everyone's like, "Oh, he's such a – You're an actor: you probably go around sleeping with everybody." So, it kind of has the reverse effect of what you would have thought.'

Despite what he was saying, gossip magazines started reporting that Rob was dating various celebrities, which he found strange. He shared with a reporter from *Showbiz Spy*: 'I am single at the moment, but I read stories in the magazines and papers that I am dating so-and-so. But it's not true. But they are very good guesses because I always fancy the girl they pair me up with. I'm hoping it's the girl herself who has made it up – then I'm in with a real chance. Maybe I should start getting in touch with them!'

He found the story about him taking *Transformers*' star Megan Fox out for a date very odd as they had only stood together for photos at the 2009 Teen Choice Awards and that had been all the contact he'd had with her. His friends back in London had believed the rumours at first and had texted him about it to get the inside scoop.

Rob enjoyed visiting different countries to promote *Twilight* but often his visits were very brief and involved long days filled with interview after interview. He found himself getting emotional on his way to Italy, telling *Frida* magazine: 'I landed in London recently, on my way to Rome, and I almost cried because I missed it so much. And I miss my dog. I haven't moved here [to Los Angeles] for good. I live in a rented apartment, where all of the furniture is rented.'

Despite feeling homesick at times he did enjoy the experience of visiting countries he had never been to before. He especially liked promoting the movie in Japan. In the country's capital, Tokyo, he could just blend into the crowd and not be recognised. In a video interview, he revealed: 'I did go to Tokyo the other day, doing more press stuff, and no one recognised me and it was the first time in a year. It was amazing; it was absolutely incredible! I could go in fast-food restaurants and no one knows who you are.

'I was kinda shocked how apparently in Japan girls hate facial hair on Westerners, but they don't mind it on Japanese people. It's like really odd. They were very adamant that I had to be clean-shaven for all of the interviews.'

During his flight over to Japan he'd been spotted by *X-Men* star Hugh Jackman, who was also on the flight as he was travelling with director Baz Luhrmann to promote their movie, *Australia*. After they landed, they decided to go for a drink together and ended up doing a late-night karaoke session.

Hugh explained how a Japanese karaoke works to MTV:

'The first thing you do is you get inside this room, the doors are closed, and there's, like, eight of you…So it feels a little weird. And then all of a sudden, they open, and they bring in these boxes, which are basically [full of] dress-up [clothes], and it's all girls' clothes. I was a schoolgirl, Baz got dressed up, and Rob did not. He was too cool for school.'

Hugh was blown away with how soulful Rob's voice was. Even though they'd had a drink, Rob put in a great performance. It had been ages since he'd sung in front of strangers, as he'd had to give up performing at open mic nights once he started getting recognised by *Twilight* fans. He used to perform under the stage name Bobby Dupea but once fans started recording him and putting the videos on YouTube he'd had to stop because it took the enjoyment out of it for him.

> **DID YOU KNOW?**
> Rob is a massive Jack Nicholson fan and for his stage name decided to use the name of Jack Nicholson's character in the 1970 movie *Five Easy Pieces* (his favourite Nicholson movie). He also set up a secret MySpace account under the name Bobby Dupea but when the Twilight Lexicon fan site found it and shared it with the world he changed the settings to private so no one could listen to the tracks he had posted on there.

When he'd lived in London he'd actually been in a band called Bad Girls, but they never released a record. He told one journalist, back in 2008: 'Bad Girls belonged to my first girlfriend's current boyfriend and he was having an open mic night. He invited me to sing, but it was just a bit of fun. We only played a couple of gigs. It is just a couple of friends of mine and some other people that I had met fairly recently – we just wanted to start a band for something to do. A lot of my friends are actors and we had so little to do all the time, so instead of just being bored, we were like, "Why not start a band?" So we did. I had kind of roll-on, roll-off musicians. I still try and play, but it's weird now since when I'm trying to do it as an actor, it always seems kind of cheesy.'

Music has always been something Rob has done for fun and he's never wanted to follow in his sister Lizzy's footsteps and try to make a career out of it. He started to learn to play the piano at three years old and took up the guitar when he was five. During his time in London he became a pianist and played at a few pizza restaurants. He found playing for people very relaxing.

DID YOU KNOW?

Rob once described his musical style as being a bit like his two favourite artists, Van Morrison and Jeff Buckley. He loves music, but prefers classic songs from blues legends John Lee Hooker and Elmore James over modern-day hits.

CHAPTER 10

STAYING TRUE TO HIMSELF

Rob's sudden popularity after *Twilight* was released meant that he was in demand on the celebrity circuit – with lots of people wanting to benefit from his fame. He had to be very careful when it came to choosing his friends, wondering if people were just inviting him to things because he was famous or because they genuinely liked him.

He wasn't interested in hangers-on and tended to spend his free time with Kristen and the rest of the *Twilight* cast. At the same time, he made sure he didn't neglect the friends he had had before moving to America. Despite living thousands of miles away from Marcus Foster, Bobby Long and Sam Bradley, he still considered them his best friends.

Back when he lived in London, they would write songs and perform together, for their own amusement. During *Twilight* filming, Catherine Hardwicke somehow managed to get her hands on a copy of their recordings and was so impressed that she decided to use two of the songs. Rob didn't know anything about it until he went to see an early version of the movie. He explained to Gina McIntyre from *Hero Complex* at the time: 'When I went to see the cut she'd put these two songs in. They're old songs, but one of them specifically, it really made the scene better. It was like it was supposed to be there. It's strange because what was supposed to be at that point in the movie was a big orchestral film climax. Instead it's this little song with acoustic guitar. I'm singing it, maybe that makes it different, but it's kind of overwhelming. I hope it's overwhelming.'

Rob had never intended for his music to be heard by Catherine and hoped that fans would recognise this and not presume he was trying to get a recording deal, explaining that, 'I really didn't want it to look like I was trying to cash in. I hope it doesn't come across as that. I'm not going to be doing any music videos or anything. Music is my backup plan if acting fails. I don't want to put all my eggs in one basket.'

By including 'Never Think' and 'Let Me Sign' on the *Twilight* soundtrack Catherine wasn't just introducing the wider world to Rob's musical talents but she was also showcasing how talented Sam, Bobby and Marcus were too. Rob had written 'Never Think' with Sam and 'Let Me Sign' had been written by Bobby and Marcus two years earlier. Rob and his mates could never have imagined something so wonderful would have come of their jamming sessions on the roof of Rob's flat in Soho. Back then, they would hang out until five in the morning, watching films, eating pizza, drinking and making music together.

The album debuted at number one on the Billboard 200 charts when it was released on 4 November 2008 and sold an incredible 165,000 copies in the USA in its first week. It went on to become Atlantic Records' best-selling soundtrack ever. As well as topping the USA charts it was number one in New Zealand and Greece, number two in Australia and Mexico, number three in Italy and did well in other countries too.

> **DID YOU KNOW?**
>
> When Rob found out his songs would be appearing on the soundtrack he initially didn't want to put his name to them, revealing to *Fandango*: 'I had thought it would be quite cool to have it be a secret thing and not have my name in the credits, like a marketing gimmick. It was nice, and also helped my friends as well.'

All three of Rob's song-writing buddies were thrilled when *Twilight* did so well and made Rob a huge star. Bobby told *Celebuzz* at the time: 'This is the best person all of this could ever happen to. It would never affect Robert the wrong way – he's exactly as he always was. He's very down-to-earth and humble, just a normal lad.'

They felt very privileged to be invited to the LA and London premieres and having the opportunity to walk down the red carpet.

For Rob, becoming one of the most in-demand actors in the world was extremely hard for him to take in. He wasn't used to being the centre of attention. When he was asked to present at the Oscars on 22 February 2009, he thought it must be a joke. He hadn't expected to get an invite, let alone be asked to present alongside the lovely star of *Mamma Mia!* Amanda Seyfried. He had never been a public speaker so just having the confidence to speak in front of so many people was going to be a huge challenge.

As he made his way into the Kodak Theater, Los Angeles, Rob felt really nervous on the red carpet – he'd messed up the rehearsal and thought he was going to be the biggest let-down in Oscar history. A few hours later, when it was all over, he reflected on how well it had gone and how it hadn't been quite as scary as he'd imagined to stand up on the stage and introduce a montage of the romantic movies of 2008. To the 36 million people watching at home, he appeared relaxed.

He confessed to *Fandango*: 'I got there and then I'm sitting in the second row. It was unbelievable – I keep thinking that something terrible is going to happen. "Death" is the only thing I'm thinking the whole time. I just used up all my luck, so I'm probably going to die at 23 or something.'

Viewing figures for the Oscars went up by 4 million from the previous year and many felt it was down to the younger stars like Rob, Amanda, Zac Efron and Freida Pinto being invited to present. They had brought a new audience to the show and many predicted that another batch of young stars would be invited to present the following year.

> **DID YOU KNOW?**
> Kristen and Taylor were invited to present the Horror films montage at the 2010 awards. Other presenters included Miley Cyrus, Chris Pine and Anna Kendrick (who plays Jessica Stanley in the *Twilight* movies).

His co-star Ashley Greene, who played Alice Cullen, gave *OK! Magazine* an insight into what the real Rob is like shortly after *Twilight* was released and his fame rocketed. She admitted: 'He's not the most sociable. He's not one of those people who can go and talk to anyone. He's kind of a hermit and a little awkward. He got thrust into this limelight, but he's dealing with it. I think it'd be kind of difficult for anyone.'

Rob's schedule around the release was crazy but when he did eventually get a chance to go back to Barnes and stay at his childhood home he must have felt like everything was a dream when he woke up in his old bedroom. He has admitted in the past that he has spent so little time there that it hasn't changed much since he was ten.

Twilight's success turned Rob's life upside down. Everywhere he went paparazzi followed him, eager to get a photograph him doing everyday tasks like running errands and buying coffee. People had become obsessed with his hair, which he found strange because his hairstyle had never gotten much attention in the past. He didn't spend time styling it and if anything, it was a bit neglected because he hardly ever washed it. He just woke up in the morning and left it as it was.

This love for his hair stemmed from interviews he had done where fans had noticed how he runs his hands through his hair subconsciously. They found it incredibly sexy and loved how he didn't always realise he was doing it. They started complaining when he wore hats and during one video interview in New York, 95 per cent of people who texted in to ask a question asked him to take his hat off. He was flabbergasted that people cared so much as his hairstyle wasn't anything special in his eyes as lots of men his age in London had the exact same style.

DID YOU KNOW?
When Rob was a child he used to hate his dad brushing his hair.

Many fans loved his hairstyle because it was the same hairstyle he had in *Twilight*. When Rob wore a hat he didn't look as much like Edward and many fans didn't like that. The most obsessed fans sometimes failed to see Rob and Edward as two separate entities. If Catherine Hardwicke's plans to have Rob wear a wig to play Edward had come to fruition then maybe his hair wouldn't have been such a big talking point among the *Twilight* fan base and the wider world.

Before they'd started filming *Twilight* she'd made Rob trial a long wig but it just hadn't looked right. She explained in her *Director's Notebook*, which came out in March 2009: 'I thought he would look good with long, "timeless" hair, so Rob spent eight hours in the chair. Nicole Frank, assistant hairstylist, put in extensions. Rob *hated* them! The next day, Nicole yanked them out, and she and Mary Ann and Rob started working on the now-famous Edward hairstyle.'

In December 2008, Rob was fed up with all the attention his hair was getting and decided to have it cut. The crew-cut look didn't go down too well with many fans but it quickly grew out and he had his trademark hair back.

Rob might have cut his hair despite knowing that fans wouldn't like it but that didn't mean he didn't value their opinions. He dedicated a lot of his spare time to reading the fan mail he was sent, and replying to as many letters as he could. He loved unwrapping the gifts he received and seeing the scrapbooks fans had made him, but his popularity meant that it could take up to six months for fans to receive a response.

He told the *Los Angeles Times* at the time: 'I go through

it myself [fan mail], but I think I might get them censored, because I'm always expecting to get the one thing that says, "I know where you live and I'm going to kill you!" I'm always expecting that to come, but it never seems to arrive.' He told the *Los Angeles Times* back in 2008, 'I never get any negative mail, so someone must be censoring them.

'I get a ton of letters. There was kind of a steady stream since *Harry Potter* but then as soon as [*Twilight*] came out…every week, there's like thousands more than there was before.'

He has always hated his first name so when fans gave him the nicknames RPattz and Spunk Ransom he didn't mind, but he would have preferred something else. When he was asked by MTV about how he felt at being called Spunk Ransom he replied, 'At least it's not an insult – it sounds kind of like antacid or something. Spunk, there's a girl called Ransom…I'd like to be called "Randsom Spunk" or "Spunk Ransom."'

He felt guilty for not having the time to stop and chat to fans he met on a day-to-day basis. 'You have to rush through everything so much. I just feel terrible every single time because people have queued up since 4 o'clock in the morning for five seconds, and that's it,' he told CBS Channel 11.

But he did find it strange when the odd fan approached him with a bleeding neck and asked him to bite them. Some mothers even requested that he should bite their babies. He told *E! Online* about one incident with a seven-year-old fan: 'She went really quiet and she was like, "Can you bite me?"

It wasn't a joke…I looked at her and thought, "Do you know what you're saying?"'

During the *Twilight* promotional tour he admitted that when groups of fans start screaming at him it makes him feel nervous. On one such occasion in Italy it even made him cry. He found it so embarrassing that Kristen noticed his reaction but at the end of the day, he just couldn't help himself, the tears started falling. In an attempt to reduce the amount of screaming from fans on his days off, he started going out wearing disguises to try and go incognito. He would wear sunglasses, a hat and put his hood up to try to hide his identity.

DID YOU KNOW?
It isn't just screaming girls that makes Rob feel nervous. He doesn't like flying, he has to sleep with a light on because he's scared of the dark and he's scared someone will stab him one day.

Rob has always struggled with crowds but it became a bigger issue for him when he started getting mobbed by fans. He explained to a journalist from *Girlfriend* magazine: 'I've been uncomfortable in crowds my whole life. I've always felt that everyone is looking at me [laughs]. So this doesn't make any difference. I could be in a supermarket and have a full-on panic attack when there's no one else there. And this was even like five years ago when nobody knew who I was!'

He added to *Collider.com*: 'My brain doesn't really accept fame so it's fine. I can be put anywhere and it just goes completely over my head. I just don't want to get shot or stabbed. I don't want someone to have a needle and I'll get AIDS afterwards, that's my only real fear. Whenever I see a crowd, I always think that. It's like being on a plane: I think the bottom is going to hit the runway when it's taking off.'

CHAPTER 11

THE NEXT CHAPTER

Pretty much as soon as *Twilight* was released fans speculated that Rob and Kristen were more than just good friends. Rob had never been romantically linked to anyone famous before so it was a new experience for him. On 31 May 2009, after they went up on stage to accept their award for Best Kiss at the MTV Movie Awards, Rob went to kiss Kristen but she pulled away, much to the surprise of everyone in the Gibson Amphitheatre and watching at home.

After the event Rob admitted that he knew Kristen would pull away because they had planned for it to happen. The fake kiss was all her idea.

Fans came to the conclusion that if Rob and Kristen weren't actually dating then they had the kind of close friendship that not many people find in their whole lifetimes. In their *Twilight* promotional interviews they displayed real admiration for each other, they seemed to want to praise each other rather than talk about their own acting abilities. Rob constantly told reporters Kristen was the best actress of their generation and she was the reason why he wanted to do *Twilight*. In turn, Kristen told reporters that Rob was her perfect Edward – really handsome, sensitive and a great actor.

> DID YOU KNOW?
> They would go on to win the Best Kiss Award at the following three MTV Movie Awards!

Kristen declared to *The Advertiser*: 'We went through a lot together. It is crazy to go through something that heavy in real life. At the end of it you are inevitably going to have something. I know a version of him better than anybody else in the world because I did this movie [*Twilight*] with him.'

Originally, both *Twilight* author Stephenie Meyer and Catherine Hardwicke herself were keen for Catherine to direct *New Moon*, but they had to wait and see how *Twilight* did at the box office. When it was announced that *New Moon* was to be made, fans assumed Catherine would be at the helm – but they were wrong.

In fact, Catherine was offered the opportunity to direct *New Moon*, but she turned the job down. The studio were keen for the film to come out as soon as possible to maximise sales so wanted it to be ready for release in November 2009. Although Catherine knew the books inside out, and had already gained a strong connection with *Twilight* fans, the actors themselves and author Stephenie Meyer, she didn't think that she could make a good movie in the given time.

She confessed to *EW.com* that despite being offered 'more money than [she] or anyone in [her] family had ever seen' for the second *Twilight* movie, she decided to say no and give someone else the opportunity to direct Rob, Kristen and the rest of the cast.

Rob, Kristen and Taylor Lautner (who played Jacob Black) had already signed a contract saying they would play Edward, Bella and Jacob in *New Moon* and *Eclipse* if they were ever made, but with *Twilight* doing so well they decided it was time to negotiate. By sticking together they had a lot more power as there was no way the studio could replace all three main stars. Because of the success of *Twilight* (it took over $392 million worldwide at the box office alone), Rob was due to receive a retroactive bonus of £300,000, however, during negotiations for *New Moon* his *Twilight* contract was amended to include an additional retroactive bonus – giving him an extra $2.5 million.

Once he knew *New Moon* was going to be made Rob was determined to improve on his *Twilight* performance, even though his fans thought he did incredibly well. He watched the movie again and again, analysing every scene he was in and making notes. In many ways, Rob is a perfectionist when it comes to his work, he always wants to do things better. Because Edward Cullen wasn't the central character in *New Moon*, he knew he would have more freedom to implement the changes he wanted to make.

Chris Weitz was the man brought in to direct *New Moon* once it became clear that Catherine Hardwicke wouldn't be returning. He had just finished directing Nicole Kidman and Daniel Craig in the children's fantasy adventure movie *The Golden Compass*.

When Chris had first been approached by the studio he hadn't read the books or even watched *Twilight* because he had wrongly presumed it was a movie just for young girls to go and see. Once he watched it himself he realised it appealed to a much wider audience and was excited to be given the opportunity to work with Rob and the rest of the relatively young cast.

The studio felt that Chris was the perfect man to take over from Catherine Hardwicke and set him the challenge of trying to make the second movie just as popular as the first. They had recognised that Rob had been a major factor in why *Twilight* was such a success and had come to the conclusion that he needed a larger role in *New Moon* than had been presented in Stephenie Meyer's book. In order to achieve this Chris decided to have Edward appear in Bella's hallucinations rather than her just hearing his voice, as had been the case in the book. This would give him more screen time, hopefully satisfying his fans.

The decision was also made to move filming from Portland in the USA to Vancouver, Canada for a number of reasons. The production team didn't feel that Portland could cope with *New Moon* and the third movie *Eclipse* potentially being filmed back-to-back and the lower Canadian dollar made Vancouver a cheaper option. A lot of work had to go into finding substitute locations and recreating some of the buildings that had already appeared in *Twilight*.

Although Rob had enjoyed working with Catherine Hardwicke and learnt so much from her, he was excited to get the opportunity to work with Chris and to film what was his favourite book in Stephenie Meyer's saga. He felt that the real Edward is revealed in *New Moon* rather than the idealistic one portrayed in *Twilight*.

He discussed his viewpoint with *Film.com*, saying: 'In the second one, he [Edward] makes a mistake that's acknowledged by everybody, including himself. Also, he is totally undermined by more powerful creatures, and he's undermined emotionally by people as well. That's what humanised it. Since I read that book, I always liked him as a character, and I've tried to play that same feeling throughout the films. He's the hero of the story that just refuses to accept that he's the hero, and I think that's kind of admirable.'

Rob really enjoyed working with Chris on *New Moon*. He

liked the way that the director was very calm and focused the whole time and he enjoyed reading the detailed syllabus that Chris gave each cast member shortly before filming started. It was clear that he was passionate about character development and wanted to bring out the best in every actor and actress in the cast.

And Rob told Rebecca Murray from *About.com* about the syllabus Chris provided: 'I've never had that, from any director. It was 40 or 50 pages long, in addition to a bunch of letters and emails, trying to show that he was on the same page as us and was completely with us, in making the film. And he didn't falter from that attitude throughout the whole movie. It probably sounds ridiculous how much praise he gets. I was just with him and his wife in Japan, and she was even kind of sick of it, but he is like a saint. He's one of the best people I've ever met, let alone directors. In a lot of ways, it shows in the movie. It's got a lot of heart, especially for a sequel in a franchise. He's just a great person to work with.'

Once they started working together Rob realised that he and Chris shared a similar sense of humour so they could bounce off each other and have fun. They connected well socially, but also professionally. They enjoyed such a good relationship during the filming of *New Moon* that Chris allowed Rob to halt filming at times and discuss at length how he felt some of the scenes might be improved. Chris chatted to the *Los Angeles Times* about one such scene in which Edward is talking to Aro.

Rob sensed it wasn't going right so stopped filming in order to discuss the matter with Chris.

Chris revealed: 'I promised the actors that no matter what, we would have time to discuss every single line. There was a line that he felt was repetitive and Rob wasn't feeling where he was in the scene. We worked it out and came up with some alternative dialogue. I can work on the fly a bit because I'm a writer-director, which is helpful. I don't feel stuck or panicky when an actor is not down with a particular piece of dialogue.'

Rob found the break-up scene a challenge because he'd never dumped a girl before. He'd always been the one to be dumped once a girl became bored with him. When asked in one interview with *OK! Magazine* what it was like to film the break-up, he replied: 'There's something weird about it. One of the main things I felt doing that, and what really helped was people's anticipation of the movie and the fans of the series' idea about what Bella and Edward's relationship is, and what it represents to them. It's some kind of ideal for a relationship. And so, just playing a scene where you're breaking up the ideal relationship, I felt a lot of the weight behind that. Also, it took away a fear of melodrama. It felt seismic, even when we were doing it. It was very much like the stepping out into the sunlight scene at the end. You could really feel the audience watching as you're doing it – it was a strange one to do.'

Rob enjoyed filming in Vancouver and would often go out for dinner with Kristen and other members of the cast and crew. It was nice to relax after a hard day on set and they enjoyed being in each other's company. They would sign autographs for fans who approached them and didn't feel under threat, however, this may have changed after 10 May 2009.

That particular night, they had come outside to get a taxi back to the hotel and were ushered into a waiting limo. Once inside the driver whisked them away before anyone could tell them that he wasn't an authorised limo driver. He had just been a fan wanting to spend some time with Rob and Kristen and had been circling the block in the hope that he could convince them to take a ride with him. He didn't harm them at all and did drop them off at their hotel but, at the same time, what would have happened if he had wanted to harm them? If anything, it was a rookie mistake: stars like Angelina Jolie and Brad Pitt would never step into a car without knowing for sure who was driving it. Rob and Kristen had become millionaires after their contract negotiations and perhaps it was time for them to start thinking about their personal safety more.

This wasn't the first time Rob had seen fans go to extraordinary lengths in order to spend time with him. When he had been filming *Little Ashes* in Spain he had been faced with having a stalker, who had stood outside his apartment every day for weeks. In the end, Rob decided to go out for dinner with her and was surprised to find it made her lose interest in him and she didn't come back. He thought he might have put her off by complaining too much about his life but maybe she had achieved all that she had hoped for, she had just wanted the opportunity to spend time with him.

Another stalker found his LA apartment and started leaving notes on his car, demanding that he spoke to her. At first the notes were friendly, asking him to call her, but as each day passed, they become more and more aggressive. One note said that she was going to kill herself if Rob didn't speak to her. It must have been hard for him to read something like that and even harder to decide what to do.

Rob was given two personal bodyguards for his own protection when Chris Weitz decided to take him, Kristen, Ashley Greene and a few other members of the *New Moon* cast to Italy for three intense weeks of filming in May in order to film the Volturi scenes. This was by no means a holiday for any of the cast or crew, although they did take time out to celebrate Rob's twenty-fifth birthday on 13 May.

Filming the scenes became a huge challenge once Italian *Twilight* fans' sites broke the news that they were filming in Montepulciano, Southern Tuscany. Literally thousands of fans from all around the world turned up in the medieval town in the hills to watch Rob and co. The movie's production team had originally signed up thousands of local people to don red capes and be extras during the Feast of Saint Marcos scenes, but after some dropped out they invited some fans to take their place. Being an extra wasn't at all glamorous, filming took many hours, it was very hot under the cloaks and everyone taking part was doing it for free so it's no wonder really that some people quit.

Chris revealed at a *New Moon* press conference: 'Everywhere where the camera wasn't pointed, there were hundreds of fans there. And it wasn't so much that we minded them being there, it was great. As a matter of fact, people applauded after every take, which is unheard of – it was like doing theatre or something. But it was the sheer logistics of getting through all the fans to get through to where we had to stand by the camera.

'There was one moment where I really had to go to the bathroom, but there was not one single cafe that I could walk into where I wouldn't be mobbed. And by the way, it's not because I'm me, but it's because people were interested if I could set up a meeting with Rob or another member of the cast. So that was quite difficult, actually, but also intriguing and fun in the same way.'

Rob might have been getting used to girls screaming every time they saw him but he still had body issues and wasn't confident when it came to stripping off for the scene where Edward steps into the light and Bella runs through the fountain. He felt like he was doing a striptease. Some extras watching the filming noticed how shy he was – he kept ducking into the shadows every time Chris Weitz shouted 'Cut!' He didn't enjoy being half-naked so in the end, Chris used a lorry to block out the extras' view so that Rob could just relax without feeling self-conscious.

It was during this time that Rob began to fully understand what the fans feel for Edward and why they found the scene really emotional. He explained to *About.com*: 'Just taking that one step into the light, it's been the one moment, since the first Comic-Con, where I've felt the whole weight of anticipation and responsibility to all the people who are so obsessed with the stories. It was a good moment. It was very nerve-wracking, but I probably felt the most in character that I've ever felt, throughout the whole series, at that moment.'

DID YOU KNOW?

A make-up artist painted on Rob's chest so that he would look like he had a six-pack. She added shadows so that his muscles would appear more defined.

Rob, Kristen and Ashley still managed to have a great time despite not being able to walk anywhere. They each had two bodyguards and were picked up and driven to the set because so many fans were on the hunt for Rob. Some fans even camped outside their hotel gate. Timing was so tight that Rob only had half an hour for lunch each day and so he couldn't go round signing autographs, either.

CHAPTER 12

CAN'T STOP

Only a few weeks after *New Moon* filming finished Rob had to jet to New York to play the rebellious Tyler Hawkins in the romantic drama *Remember Me*. To have to say goodbye to Edward for a time (as well as Kristen) must have been strange, as his world had been consumed by *Twilight* for so long.

He was going to be staying in a luxury suite at The Waldorf Towers, in Midtown so invited his sister Lizzy and good friend Tom Sturridge to fly in from London to keep him company. His other friends would have come but they couldn't afford the flight over and Rob didn't want to seem pretentious by offering to pay for them.

Remember Me was another Summit Entertainment picture and his love interest in the movie was Australian actress

Emilie de Ravin. Emilie was best known for playing Claire Littleton in the TV series *Lost*. The filming schedule was tight as Rob had to be ready to film *Eclipse* in August and as soon as filming wrapped it would be time to promote *New Moon*, which was being released in November. Many fans wondered why he decided to do the movie as he could have given himself a well-deserved break instead, but Rob wanted to keep busy. He wanted to have the opportunity to play another part, to be someone other than Edward. He also knew he could learn a lot from Will Fetters, who was directing the production.

In the movie Rob's character Tyler is very troubled. He has a strained relationship with his father (played by Pierce Brosnan) and his life is going nowhere until he starts a relationship with Ally (Emilie's character). Playing him allowed Rob to develop a character with lots of light and shade.

Some fans wrongly thought Rob was on a date with Emilie when they were spotted hanging out in the Los Angeles County Museum of Art (LACMA). Rob was looking every inch the model in a designer suit, which should have been a giveaway sign that he was working, since he likes to dress inconspicuously when he's out and about, opting for nondescript hoodies, T-shirts and casual trousers. He would much prefer to blend into the background rather than stand out.

The fans tried to get a closer look, but the rooms Rob and Emilie were in were cordoned off and security guards were placed at all the entrances. Later, it was revealed that they had been there to do a photo shoot for *Vogue* to promote *Remember Me*.

DID YOU KNOW?

Rob didn't have time to get his own clothes laundered while he was in New York so just boxed up his dirty washing and sent it to his hotel room in Vancouver to sort out later. Weeks passed before he eventually got round to getting them cleaned because he was so busy with *Eclipse*.

It wasn't just fans who jumped to the wrong conclusion about Rob and Emilie, the media did too. When they filmed a kissing scene on a New York beach, paparazzi captured the moment and the sensational photos were soon published worldwide. When fans saw the photos of Rob and Emilie lying in the sand together many wondered how Kristen might feel on seeing him kissing another woman, although she herself wouldn't have had a problem with it because she would have known it was just part and parcel of being an actor.

Many fans were convinced that Kristen and Rob were secretly dating, even though Kristen was supposed to be in a relationship with actor Michael Angarano at the time.

But it wasn't just Emilie that Rob had kissed since leaving Kristen's side. Just a few weeks earlier he had kissed two fans at a charity event. Rob has always been a huge supporter of charity work and since becoming famous he has done his utmost to help worthy causes.

Rob had been at the Cannes Film Festival alongside some of the biggest stars on the planet. Brad Pitt, Jim Carrey and Ben Stiller were all present, treading the red carpet and promoting their up-and-coming movies. Rob was there to promote *New Moon* by himself and found having to pose for endless photos by the harbourside rather awkward. He would have found it much more enjoyable if he'd had Kristen, Taylor or any of the other members of the cast with him. Visiting Cannes had always been a dream of Rob's but he really wished to make a movie good enough to be screened there.

In some interviews he found himself digressing and talking about things other than *New Moon*. He revealed to the Z100 radio station that his sisters Lizzy and Victoria can be a bit overprotective and quiz his female friends: 'I caught my sister saying to someone the other day, and she's a friend of mine as well, "Why do you like my brother? Like, is it just…do you like him because he's in movies?" And she's like, "You know what he is, he's just a really lying guy, he's a terrible person."'

Rob might have turned twenty-three that week but his sisters still wanted to look out for him. They were wary of women who tried to get close to him, even though he himself often encouraged them, 'I have a very specific idea of how to be around women and stuff, but I mean I've never understood the point of hanging out with guys. What is the point?' he mused.

While he was in Cannes there was the annual amfAR Cinema Against AIDS 2009 Cocktail Party. There was to be an auction and Rob would take part. It was down to American film producer and movie studio chairman Harvey Weinstein to announce what was going to happen. He told those gathered: 'When I first saw *Twilight* with my daughters, I went home the next night and I saw [written] on their doors, Emma Pattinson age eleven, Ruby Pattinson age six and Lily Pattinson age fourteen. All three of my daughters want to marry the guy on my right – I want him to star in a movie for me!'

Rob had to try and not look too embarrassed while Harvey continued: '[He] has agreed to do something extraordinary…I think there is no dad who wouldn't mind Robert Pattinson meeting his daughter, taking a picture with his daughter and just giving her a gentle kiss on the cheek. Somebody in London, New York or LA, there's got to be a dad good enough to bid on that!'

Basic Instinct actress Sharon Stone was hosting the night and also in charge of the auction for Rob's kiss. Before she started the bidding off, Rob jokingly suggested that it should start at $5. As more and more bids came in, everyone began to realise that the kiss was going to raise an amazing amount for charity. In the end, the bidding got so heated that Rob said he would kiss the daughters of the two remaining bidders if they each gave $20,000. The parents agreed to this and the lucky girls got their kisses!

Emilie de Ravin was asked to compare working with Rob with the actors she'd previously worked with in *Lost* during the TCA (Television Critics Association) press tour in January 2010. She told the gathered journalists: 'Every experience with whoever you work with is always different. I had a great time working with him – we really made a point of working on our characters and their relationships and such. He's a really easy-going and nice guy to work with, which is always refreshing.'

For Rob, playing Tyler in *Remember Me* was a great experience but because it was by the same studio as the *Twilight* movies he wasn't sure of his economic viability outside of playing Edward. He knew that Summit Entertainment rated him but once the *Twilight* movies were over, would other studios feel the same way? Would the offers dry up? He wasn't sure and couldn't say what he would be doing five years down the line. He admitted this openly to journalists at the time, he didn't try to hide how he was feeling.

He knew his success had opened doors, he was being offered roles that he never would have been able to get an audition for in the past, but in some ways he wanted to return to the days of auditioning as a nobody. He wanted to win parts because he had given the best audition, not just because he was 'Robert Pattinson'.

Rob admitted to *About.com*: 'Before *Twilight*, I did any movie that I got and tried to make the best of it afterwards. Now, you're expected to come into the movie and provide not only economic viability, but a performance as well. People are like, "You can't just mess around: we're employing you to be a star and an actor." It's difficult and it's scary.'

The downside to Rob's success was that he was constantly being hounded by paparazzi and being accused of things that simply weren't true. He hadn't wanted this aspect of being famous to change him as a person, telling fan site *Twilight Series Theories*: 'I hope success hasn't really changed me at all. I mean, I don't feel like it has – I don't feel any different to what I did before. I guess my friends would have to judge me, but I don't feel any different.'

He hated that the paparazzi took photos of him doing everyday mundane tasks and the photos would appear online and in magazines the next day. He told *Newsbeat Entertainment*: 'I think someone follows me. They do the most random stuff – I get a photo taken through a burger drive-through window and it's like, "What?" They always seem like they're six feet away. I don't understand. I'm walking around and I don't see anybody.'

Some bloggers and gossip sites even made up stories to upset Rob's fans. They didn't care how Rob or his family would feel about reading that he had died or been seriously injured in an accident. In June 2009 they had reported that Rob had narrowly avoided being hit by a taxi in New York after fans chased him onto a busy street. The rumour went global and Ashley Greene (who plays Alice in the *Twilight* movies) was asked how Rob was doing on the red carpet at an event, just a few hours later. She hadn't heard anything about the accident because there had been no accident. Rob revealed the truth to *Access Hollywood*: 'It was the most innocuous situation. I think the cab may have been stationary – I may have just walked into the cab. It was entirely blown out of proportion: they were saying there were mobs of screaming fans, there were no fans there, it was like 4 o'clock in the morning…and it was just one paparazzi who couldn't get a photo.'

To a journalist from Yahoo, Rob added: 'I also had a "heroin overdose" in New York as well, which was an exciting one for my mum. I had been working so hard, my mum calls me up so much, but I didn't answer the phone and when I found out afterwards when one of the security guys from the film came, he ran into my room and I was like, "What are you doing? You could have knocked!" It was on a very legitimate news source, so bizarre.

'The thing is, people read it. I'm so ignorant I just think, "No one reads this stuff anyway, I'm the only one who reads it." Sometimes you get quite frustrated by it…everything goes away.'

Rob has yet to take a publication to court for printing lies about him but may well change his mind in the future. Once, when he was asked at a press conference what was the weirdest or funniest thing he'd ever read or heard about himself, he teased: 'Recently, some magazine had on the cover that I was pregnant. I was just like, "Wow!" And, it was without a hint of irony or anything. I didn't really know what to make of that one. I don't even know if that qualifies as libellous because they can just say, "Well, it's obviously fiction," but it's written in a non-fiction magazine. I saw a couple of comments under the article saying, "That's why he always wears jackets. He always wears layers to hide it."'

To try to protect himself he did start saying no to interviews with certain magazines because they kept printing stories that portrayed him as having a problem with alcohol. Rob hated being exploited just so magazines could sell more copies. He also started spending more time in private, where the paparazzi couldn't photograph him, so would hang out in his hotel room as opposed to spending time in a bar or café. He figured it was the best thing to do in the short term but didn't want it to become a long-term solution. He didn't want to become a recluse, he wanted to enjoy life.

The press's obsession with Rob's private life upset his family in 2009, after magazines printed quotes allegedly from his aunt. Rob's mum was angry. This really upset Monica, who told her local paper, the *Dorking and Leatherhead Advertiser*: 'It was very scary to have someone on your doorstep at all times of the day and night, firing off questions as mad as "What size are his feet?" and "What colour socks does he wear?"

'I even contacted Sir Paul Beresford, our local MP, about the intrusion and he told me it was just the freedom of the press – I was at my wits' end.'

Regarding the magazine article that caused the family rift she said: 'They were completely made-up quotes. Whenever anyone came to my door I would always say "no comment", so I was really upset to see the article, which was obscene.'

CHAPTER 13

BACK TO EDWARD

It was all change again for the third movie with *Hard Candy*'s David Slade taking over as director. Chris Weitz would have loved to have directed *Eclipse* but it wasn't possible because he would still be doing *New Moon*'s post-production while *Eclipse* was due to be filmed. The studio wanted *Eclipse* to be in cinemas seven months after *New Moon* so David was brought in.

Fans were surprised at the studio's choice as David had filmed some pretty dark movies in the past. They wondered how he would choose to tell the story. Would he stick closely to the book or would he change things a lot?

When *Time Out* asked David whether he was surprised to have been given the job because of how violent some of his previous movies had been, he replied: 'When you go in to meet for a film you very quickly get past what you've done and get on to what you will do. They look at your craft and your ability. I'm sure there were several directors in the running who had the same skills, if not better, but I talked about my vision for the film, and before I knew it they were sending me to the set of *New Moon* to meet Rob [Pattinson] and Kristen [Stewart], then off to meet Stephenie.'

For this movie Rob was upgraded. For *Twilight* and *New Moon* he had just had a hotel room, but for *Eclipse* he was given a whole floor of a hotel to share with Kristen. Rob had become such a huge star that he needed a lot more security as fans mobbed him wherever he went. Having just a whole floor to chill out in gave him enough space to enjoy having other members of the cast around in the evenings and to take pleasure just being with Kristen too.

It was so different from the room on the thirty-something floor with no windows that he'd had while filming *New Moon*, but he still couldn't feel completely relaxed. He admitted in a London press conference: 'I was kind of trapped while filming *Eclipse*, but there's always ways and there's always places where you can disappear to – it just involves a bit more thought and you can't wander around.'

Rob had to spend a lot of time in the gym learning how to run properly before he started shooting his scenes. He explained to *Collider*: 'In the last two, I ran in a limp slash-skip, and I had to look like I could run more solidly this time. So, I spent a lot of time on a giant treadmill, like one of those wheels mice run around on, and got filmed doing it to improve my form.'

He also revealed that he struggled to keep it together when he was filming the infamous tent scene with Kristen and Taylor: 'The first time we did that tent scene, I was really freaking out. I don't know why. I think it had to do with claustrophobia because we were actually shooting in a tent. I just couldn't get it together. I kept forgetting my lines, and I was so nervous. I just wanted to punch anyone who was near me. We did about three takes, and Kristen was supposed to be asleep on the floor, and she saw that I was freaking out. Halfway through the take, she suddenly opened her eyes and was just staring at me and kept trying to make me laugh, through the entire take. It's the most serious scene in the whole movie. I just wanted to strangle her for the first two seconds, but then I could not stop laughing, the entire time. We got literally one take where it went right, and it was because of that. When I was trying to hold back, I guess it made me more alive or something.'

The fight scenes between Rob and Bryce Dallas Howard (who plays Victoria) were extremely physical. Bryce confessed to the *Mail on Sunday* that she didn't want to accidentally hurt Rob in case it made his fans hate her, saying, 'There was a lot of swiping, grabbing, throwing, tackling. It was a total brawl. Everybody had bruising. I dislocated my wrist.'

Once the cast had finished filming *Eclipse* they had to go straight into promoting *New Moon*, which was released worldwide on 20 November 2010. It was a huge hit, breaking the record at the time for the biggest midnight screening in the USA and the biggest first day. It ended up taking $709,827,462 at the box office alone.

New Moon received a score of 4.6 out of 10 from IMDb, based on 197,139 reviews. Stella Papamichael from *Digital Spy* felt like Rob's lack of screen time made the movie dull, writing: 'If the first instalment of *The Twilight Saga* was a celebration of teenage sulkiness, then this sequel positively drowns in it. As Bella, Kristen Stewart is pure "heroin chic", though it isn't drugs that means she's looking so pale; it's being dumped by her bloodsucking vampire soul-mate Edward (Robert Pattinson doing his James Dean impression) because he worries for her soul. Sigh... But it, like, totally sucks because he leaves town, which means all the girls who come to watch this movie hoping for two-plus hours of drool-worthy close-ups might feel, like, totally frustrated.'

The San Francisco Chronicle's Mick LaSalle certainly wasn't a fan of *New Moon*, writing: 'So expect this film to satisfy its fans. Everybody else, get ready for a bizarre soap opera/pageant, consisting of a succession of static scenes with characters loping into the frame to announce exactly what they're thinking. Then they spell out their personalities for us. Here is an emotionally tortured vampire. Here is a perky, friendly vampire. And don't forget the vampire who is a dedicated physician.

'Meanwhile, every so often – but never more than two or

three times per minute – one of the characters makes a point of telling the perfectly nice, perfectly average teenage protagonist (Kristen Stewart) that she is the greatest thing on Earth. Sometimes it's Dad who tells her. Sometimes it's an enemy, who still recognizes our heroine's amazing power. Most of the time, it's some ridiculously handsome teenage boy. ... And each time that happens, 500 girls in the audience scream.'

The *Mirror*'s David Edwards awarded it 3 out of 5 stars and commented: 'Strip away the supernatural element and this is really a story about frustrated passions, the kind that most teens will know all about. Perhaps that's why the saga has set so many pulses racing. *Romeo and Juliet* it ain't, but as a solid love story, *New Moon* gets the blood pumping.'

Rob does actually read reviews of all the movies he does, even if reviewers are extremely negative. He confessed to *The Huffington Post*: 'Yeah [I read reviews]. I don't quite know why. It's so difficult to figure out if you're doing the right thing. I guess there's some way of knowing after reading, sort of. But sometimes it's just incredible how opposite everything can be. It's bizarre. You learn absolutely nothing after, and you just hate bad reviews. You can't even remember the good ones.'

For Rob, Kristen and Taylor the *New Moon* promotional tour involved doing hundreds of interviews around the world. They had already done some earlier promotion in the summer, and going to Comic-Con with Chris Weitz had been a particular highlight for Rob. They had been able to show fans two scenes from *New Moon* and hear their reactions to it, four months before its release. Some fans had camped for a week to get a ticket to the *New Moon* press conference, they were desperate to see Rob and hear him answer questions about the movie. Rob had been joined on stage by Chris, Kristen and Taylor, all four of them excited to talk about the movie they had been busy filming a couple of months earlier.

When the time came for Chris to say why he wanted to direct the movie he jokingly told the audience: 'I've been stalking Rob Pattinson for the last ten years, so when I got a chance to get within touching distance of him, I jumped at the opportunity…Actually, I think it's really an extraordinary cast who did the first film and I was very keen to work with them. Like most people of the male gender, I hadn't read *Twilight* before the film came up, but once I read it, I realised that it dealt with all those deep emotions that everyone feels: first-love and heartbreak and the ecstasy of reunion. Having been dumped so many times in my life, I felt that I could sympathise with Bella's character.'

The first scene fans were shown was the motorbike one between Bella and Jacob. They responded by screaming, but after seeing Edward unbutton his shirt to reveal his naked chest in the second scene, where Bella saves Edward, they went crazy!

Rob had expected fans to scream as they had screamed the year before when he'd come to Comic-Con with Catherine

Hardwicke to promote *Twilight* but their reaction to this scene was on another level completely.

Rob thoroughly enjoyed filming *New Moon* and promoting it, much more than he had done with *Twilight*. His *New Moon* shooting schedule had been a lot less hectic because he hadn't been in as many scenes. He explained to the press: 'There's been a bunch of things that have made it easier. One thing, it's my favourite book. I understood everything about it – well, not everything but a lot of it. I had a really specific way of how I wanted to play it, which influenced the way I played the first one and the third one. The second book I really connected to really quickly, and also I had months and months from *Twilight* to ruminate on that and I'd seen it… It was nice because I knew what I wanted to fix. You do that with every job you do, you notice things that need to be fixed. I improve on that, I think it's an improvement. It was nice actually not being the lead because I could implement the changes… I think it was an older performance.'

In a separate interview with French magazine *Gold* he added: 'It wasn't just the change of director that made things very different this time. There's also the fact that this time we knew the beast, we knew a little bit more what we were dealing with.

'In this film, I have a more of a secondary role. I started three weeks after the start of filming and the first scenes I shot were many scenes of hallucinations, in which I did not say more than two words. So it was probably one of the most relaxing jobs I ever had! Chris has a very calming presence, and I feel so good with him. To have no stress from the job for three months was great. It was Taylor who had to deal with the pressure! (laughs).'

Rob didn't have any issues with filming the next movie so quickly, telling journalist Rebecca Murray: 'There's nothing really scary about the franchise itself: I like all the people I work with, I generally have very few disagreements about the script or anything while we're doing it, especially on *New Moon*. It just seemed so relaxed and easy. I've been on three different sets since 14 January. I've had like, three days off. I'm going to be on set all next year as well. I don't know what doing errands and things is really like 'cos I haven't had a sustained period of time where I've been off – I don't know how it's really changed. I still feel like I'm pretty much exactly the same, which is maybe not a good thing.'

During the *New Moon* promotional tour, Rob was open to having a laugh with his co-stars and wasn't offended when they poked fun at him in front of journalists or fans. Kellan Lutz, who played Emmett Cullen, openly shared how the cast had gone for a run together one time and Rob came last out of everyone. Ashley Greene, who played Alice Cullen, described Rob's running style as being like a mountain goat.

When MTV mentioned what Ashley had said about him Rob laughed and said, 'Mountain goat? I would have said that I run more like a cheese string! What does a mountain goat run like? That is much more athletic than the way I run. I run like a person who has just had their limbs sewn together – I'm not even like a human!'

Kristen gave Rob the nickname Flippy because she thought he looked like a penguin flapping its wings whenever he tried to do a stunt. He didn't object, telling *Harper's Bazaar*: 'You notice it in the film [*New Moon*], she looks so much more athletic than I do. And I'm supposed to be the superhero.'

While they were promoting the movie in Europe, Rob and Kristen were photographed holding hands at a Paris airport on their way to London. The media went crazy and insisted the photos proved they must be dating. The pair refused to admit anything was going on between them, however, an interview Catherine Hardwicke gave to *Time* magazine confirmed fans' suspicions. Catherine admitted to *Time*: 'I didn't have a camera in the hotel room. I cannot say. In terms of what Kristen told me directly, it didn't happen on the first movie. Nothing crossed the line while on the first film.

'I think it took a long time for Kristen to realise, "Okay, I've got to give this a go and really try to be with this person."'

She also revealed that she had warned Rob not to start a relationship with Kristen after casting him as Edward. Kristen had been just seventeen at the time and therefore considered a minor.

After the Paris photos, Kristen was very outspoken during an interview with *Entertainment Weekly* and admitted that she probably would have revealed if she was in a relationship with Rob or not, if everyone hadn't made it such a big deal. She hated how the media felt they were entitled to hound her just because she was an actress. Rob admired Kristen for her strong views, telling *Harper's Bazaar*: 'Kristen doesn't take any slack. She sticks to her guns – and that's difficult to do.' He thought she was a better judge of character than he was, adding: 'She'll decide on someone a lot quicker. She has a lot more self-esteem than I do, so she's like, "You're an idiot and I don't want to talk to you," and I'm like, "I'm an idiot too!" So I'll talk to an idiot for like three days before deciding.'

Promoting movies is something that Rob will never feel comfortable with because he doesn't enjoy having to do interviews, he just wants to act. He can't escape doing them because he is contractually obliged to do so, but at the same time he wishes he had a script to follow so that he didn't have to think on his feet. Sometimes the questions he gets asked are rather random and can leave him dumbfounded for a few seconds. He also tends to overshare and told *Harper's Bazaar*: 'I don't spend any money. The only thing I've really bought is my car, which cost $1,500 and keeps exploding. It would be nice to buy a house for my parents, but at the same time my parents are so comfortable where they live, they would probably just feel like it was a burden. I wear the same clothes every day and the only thing I used to splurge on was DVDs.'

Although no official announcement was made the fact that Rob and Kristen spent New Year's Eve 2009 together gave fans all the proof they needed. Rob had decided to whisk Kristen away to somewhere he must have thought they'd never be found – the Isle of Wight.

This small British island has a population of less than 140,000 and lies three to five miles from England's South Coast in the English Channel. Rob could have suggested a more exotic location like Barbados, where many celebrities ring in the New Year, but a beach holiday under the glare of the paparazzi didn't appeal.

He probably thought that the Isle of Wight would be one of the few places in the world that wasn't *Twilight*-obsessed and they could walk around unnoticed. However, shortly after arriving, they were spotted by a young girl outside her local supermarket. They didn't mind having their photos taken with her initially but a few hours later Rob and Kristen might have had regrets, as the photos were posted on several *Twilight* fan sites. Their holiday location was no longer a secret and soon the world's media wanted to find out what they were up to.

Despite being spotted, Rob and Kristen didn't let it ruin their fun. Instead, they went to a pub called the Spyglass Inn and then headed for a party at the Winter Gardens bar in Ventnor. It cost them £3 each to get in and they mingled with the other hundred or so locals before the big countdown. They had a really good (and cheap) night. For once, they were able to just be themselves, not having to behave like movie stars.

DID YOU KNOW?

For New Year's Eve 2010 they decided to go back to the Isle of Wight and headed for the same pub, which shows how much Rob and Kristen enjoyed their time there. They didn't want to go to a big flash party with countless celebrities and instead enjoyed spending time with good friends in relaxed surroundings.

CHAPTER 14

WORKAHOLIC

The years 2008 and 2009 had been busy for Rob but they had nothing on 2010. He was filming *Bel Ami*, *Water for Elephants* and *Breaking Dawn* pretty much back-to-back.

Rob had to move out of his comfort zone to play nineteenth-century French gigolo Georges Duroy in *Bel Ami*. The movie was an adaptation of a short story by the popular nineteenth-century French writer Guy de Maupassant. It was directed by first-time directors Declan Donnellan and Nick Ormerod, and told the tale of a penniless soldier who moves to Paris to make his fortune. He manipulates wealthy mistresses in order to rise to the top of society. Filming started in February in Budapest and London but Rob had insisted that they had a month of rehearsals first.

He had actually secured the role way back in 2008, just as

he'd won the part of Edward in *Twilight*, so the directors had had no idea how big an actor he was going to become.

Rob was playing the lead role and his mistresses were played by Uma Thurman, Christina Ricci and Kristin Scott Thomas. Christina Ricci thoroughly enjoyed working with Rob and told *Glamour* magazine: 'He is wonderful to work with and he is incredibly talented and he's lovely on set. He and I had quite a bit of fun together. We laughed a lot. We were both very self-effacing and liked to make fun of ourselves. We joked about a lot on set and just generally had a good time together.'

This made their love scenes easier to shoot, with Christina adding: 'It helps if you are with someone who you can laugh with a lot, because that way you can make fun of the situation, otherwise everything gets a bit too serious and weird.'

She admitted on *Jimmy Kimmel Live* that Rob had had a voice coach for the movie, saying: 'They hired a wonderful accent coach who coached me…and also coached him because he spent a lot of time in LA. I got to make fun of him because he's actually British and sometimes would sound like he was a Valley girl. And he made fun of me because I was trying to be British and would sometimes sound like a Valley girl.

'But really I was the problem. Sometimes we would do scenes and I'd turn to him and I would [ask], "Did that sound okay?" And he'd [say], "No."'

On 1 March, Rob had to be in New York for the premiere of *Remember Me*, which was to be released in cinemas on 12

March. *Remember Me* received a score of 7.2 out of 10 from IMDb, based on 98,192 reviews. *Digital Spy*'s Simon Reynolds thought that Rob did an excellent job, but still only awarded the movie 2 out of 5 stars, saying, 'There is a lot to admire in the film: the star is good (Pattinson will have legs when he's done with Cullen), Allen Coulter's direction is more than competent and there's a nicely-chosen turn-of-the-millennium soundtrack (Sigur Rós, Ed Harcourt, Sparklehorse), yet it's not enough to make up for the thoroughly miserable tone or contrived ending.'

Empire were equally impressed with Rob's performance, declaring: 'So the boy can act – this is the best thing he's done.' But they still only gave the movie 3 out of 5 stars.

In May, Rob started filming *Water for Elephants* in Los Angeles. He played Jacob Jankowski, a young veterinary student who joins a circus after his parents are killed in a car crash. He falls in love with Marlena (played by Reese Witherspoon), who is married to the abusive circus owner August Rosenbluth (Christoph Waltz). After discovering their affair, August tries to kill Marlena, while his henchmen beat up Jacob, but elephant Rosie saves the day and kills August.

Rob had had to put in an amazing audition to win the part as Channing Tatum (*G.I. Joe*), Emile Hirsch (*Into the Wild*) and Andrew Garfield (*Spider-Man*) had all auditioned for it. But Rob was the one chosen by director Francis Lawrence.

Having the opportunity to be in a movie set in 1930s

America was a dream come true for Rob, who told *Collider*: 'I think I've just always had a bit of an affinity for that era. I always wanted to do a movie around that time. And, I think it was just very solid, how she (author Sara Gruen) created the world there. I just wanted to be a part of it.

'There's a wildness to it. I think that's why I like that period. After that, it's just white picket fences. It just gets progressively more boring. But, it's the end of the Wild West. It's why kids still want to be cowboys, even in England.'

He thought the set was incredible, enthusing, 'I've never worked on anything so detailed. There was an embankment with a train track on the top. All the trailers were on one side, and then the circus world was on the other. Once you walked over the tracks, there would be a camera, but that was the only thing from the twenty-first century. You could stand on the tracks and look over at everything, and you were in the thirties. We were out in the middle of the desert in Fillmore, and there was nothing else around. There was an orchard. We were in the thirties. Jack Fisk, the production designer, used authentic pegs and the ropes. Every single thing which built the world was all totally real. And, authentic period underpants do actually help, as well. I actually wore them every single day. Jacqueline West, the costume designer, was unbelievable. Almost everything was real. Every pair of jeans were all from the twenties and thirties. It was crazy.'

This was the first time Rob had had to work closely with

animals, and working with Tai the elephant was understandably daunting at first, but also extremely exciting. It had been the opportunity of working with Tai that had made Rob want to do the movie before he'd even seen a script. He loved watching Gary, the elephant trainer, at work and telling Tai to sit, using the same tone that he would use to speak to a dog.

As they worked together Tai formed quite a bond with Rob but he believes it was because he gave her peppermints. He used to hide mints under his clothes so she would sniff him. Filming the movie made him feel like he was living in the 1930s at times, and he discovered that he didn't mind how much animal excrement was piled up around him, confessing: 'I don't know why I wasn't grossed out by it, at all. Because everything felt so authentic all the time, you just accept it, as part of the world. The scene where we were in that train car, there were like ten billion flies. On any other movie, I think I'd be like, "Let's just do one take!" But, I was perfectly happy to make a little mound and sit there and eat my lunch.'

DID YOU KNOW?

After they had filmed some scenes in Tennessee the cast and crew drank some moonshine (illegally distilled homemade whisky), which is something Rob will never forget. It was so strong that half the crew passed out!

Rob enjoyed working with Reese Witherspoon again, but it was strange playing her lover after playing her son in *Vanity Fair*. Kissing Reese wasn't difficult for Rob, despite her being a lot smaller than he is. He told *MoviesOnline*: 'I've got quite bad posture and she's the perfect height. I've got a big, heavy head so I just slump down and she's in the right spot naturally.'

Filming *Water for Elephants* meant that Rob wasn't available for the promotional tour of *Eclipse*, however, he did make it to the Los Angeles premiere on 24 June. He brought along his mum, dad and sisters as his special guests so they could enjoy the night together.

When Kristen was interviewed on the *Late Show* with David Letterman she was asked how the promotional tour for the movie went and she replied, 'I was with Taylor this time because Rob was working and we were able to have a lot more fun.' The audience found this hilarious but she hadn't meant anything by it, she obviously loved spending time with Rob but had enjoyed just being with Taylor this time around.

Eclipse received a score of 4.9 out of 10 from IMDb, based on 160,979 reviews. The *Mirror*'s David Edward admitted in his review: '*Eclipse* is certainly a tricky film for someone of my age and gender to review. While I could bang on about the faults – its sluggishness, the habit of getting bogged down in back stories and a climax that's over in a flash – I won't, simply because here's a film for girls in their teens. And for them, *Eclipse* more than hits the sweet spot.'

One of the movie's most positive reviews came from *The Hollywood Reporter*: 'It took three films, but *The Twilight Saga* finally nails just the right tone in *Eclipse*, a film that neatly balances the teenage operatic passions from Stephenie Meyer's novels with the movies' supernatural trappings.

'Where the first film leaned heavily on camp and the second faltered through caution and slickness, *Eclipse* moves confidently into the heart of the matter – a love triangle that causes a young woman to realize choices lead to consequences that cannot be reversed.

'Pattinson makes you forget the white make-up and weird eye contact lenses to concentrate on a person torn over his love for a woman and the sacrifice he knows she will have to make to stay with him.'

Peter Debruge wrote in his review for *Variety*: 'The pleasant surprise this time around is that the result finally feels more like the blockbuster this top-earning franchise deserves. Employing a bigger budget, better effects and an edgier director (*Hard Candy*'s David Slade), *Eclipse* focuses on what works – the stars – even as the series' parent-friendly abstinence message begins to unravel. Summer release should reap Summit's biggest yield yet.'

Rob might have missed the promotion of *Eclipse* but it wasn't long before he was reunited with his cast mates as filming for *Breaking Dawn* started in the November. Summit's decision to split *Breaking Dawn* into two didn't actually impact on the filming as both pictures were being filmed at once, as if they were one big movie. There was going to be one director and the movies would be released six months apart.

Dream Girls' director Bill Condon was the man chosen for the job and he was looking forward to the challenge of bringing Stephenie Meyer's final book in the *Twilight* series to the big screen, telling *Mania Entertainment*: 'I'm very excited to get the chance to bring the climax of this saga to life on-screen. As fans of the series know, this is a one-of-a-kind book – and we're hoping to create an equally unique cinematic experience.'

Filming took place around Baton Rouge, Louisiana, Vancouver and Pemberton, British Columbia, in the main, but the first scenes they shot were in Rio de Janeiro. The final scenes they did were the wedding scenes, which were filmed under tight security as they wanted to keep Bella's dress a secret. Filming wrapped on 15 April 2011 for most of the cast but additional honeymoon scenes were filmed on 22 April on Saint Thomas, so for Rob and Kristen, this was where they said goodbye to Edward and Bella. After the cameras stopped rolling, Rob, Kristen and the crew enjoyed cocktails on the beach and watched the sunrise.

Filming the sex scenes in *Breaking Dawn* had been quite nerve-wracking for Rob in particular, even though he'd filmed quite a few sex scenes in his other movies. He knew that *Twilight* fans expected so much. He revealed to T4, a scheduling slot for Britain's TV Channel 4: 'It's just awkward, you've got all this make-up on... for some reason whenever you've got make-up on all over your body you feel like you can't, like, feel anything. It's weird. And you can't see anything because you've got contacts in... and also you're supposed to be really graceful and elegant and expert sex-havers. And it's very difficult to show that to people. Love makers is probably better than sex-havers.'

For fans who had wondered what a child of Rob and Kristen might look like in the future they got some idea when they saw the actress who would be playing their on-screen daughter, Renesmee.

Mackenzie Foy was the lucky girl who was chosen by director Bill Condon and his casting team. She was so excited to join the cast for *Breaking Dawn*, appearing in a flash forward in the first movie before having a much larger role to play in the second.

She told *USA Today*: 'Kristen's eyes are green, just like mine. And then Rob is kind of goofy. I'm kind of goofy like Rob.'

She liked wearing Converse footwear like Kristen, something which *Twilight* fans quickly picked up on. It made them wonder if having Mackenzie around made Rob feel broody but it didn't. He told reporters when asked that he has no idea when he will have kids but he has always liked babies. He has never been faced with changing a diaper and wouldn't know what to do if he were ever asked to do one. He barely knows how to look after himself and do basic tasks like turning on a washing machine, so he's not ready for the responsibility of parenthood.

Four months into arriving on set eleven-year-old Mackenzie had decided that they needed a swear jar – with all the money going to St. Jude Children's Research Hospital. Every time a member of the cast swore in front of her, they were supposed to drop money into it. Rob believed he swore the most but that Peter Facinelli [who played Carlisle Cullen] donated the most. When Mackenzie first suggested it he thought it was a good scam – perhaps something he would have done when he was the same age to try to get money from adults.

Rob hadn't worked with many children before Mackenzie so it took a bit of adjusting to get used to her. During a Twitter event with *Glamour* magazine a fan tweeted to ask: 'What's your favourite scene with Mackenzie?' Rob answered: 'There's a scene when she runs up… and we're planning a battle and she jumps up into my arms but they're not recording sound and so I'm saying all this stuff, saying all this incredibly inappropriate stuff and she always gets really angry at me. It's really funny because it looks really sweet but…'

He was also asked if he would read *Twilight* to his future kids. He replied: 'Depends on if they want to, I don't believe in reading to kids. You put the book in front of them, if you wanna read, you've got to learn!'

It's no real surprise that Rob answered in this way as he has always been independent and liked doing things for himself, even when he was a schoolboy.

Water for Elephants was released on 22 April 2011 so Rob had to jump straight into promoting that movie as soon as he finished on *Breaking Dawn*. Kristen accompanied him to the New York premiere and after enjoying the after-party they were photographed kissing in the back seat of a car.

The media seemed very keen to suggest that Rob and his leading lady in the movie, Reese Witherspoon, weren't the best of friends, since both of them seemed rather glum at the Paris premiere, but they were probably just jetlagged. The media claimed that Rob had been upset when Reese divulged in an interview that their love scenes hadn't been enjoyable because Rob had a runny nose. He set the record straight in an interview with the *Chicago Sun Times*: 'Listen, I had a cold and kept apologising to Reese, who has since revealed to the press that I had the worst sinus infection when I was kissing her. She has said, "He was just sniffing all the way through." I guess that was her response to, "Reese, you're the envy of so many girls." I shouldn't have made my nose run. I was so embarrassed.'

While promoting the movie in Sydney they were upstaged by an elephant, which promptly relieved itself on the pavement. Rob told the gathered journalists about the first time he had met Tai, explaining: 'Francis Lawrence [the director] said he wanted to have a meeting and he took me out to the elephant sanctuary, where Tai [who plays Rosie the elephant] lives, and

I saw her doing a handstand and stayed there for about four hours, playing catch with her.

'I would literally throw a ball and she would catch it in her trunk and throw it back to me, and I was like, "OK, even if this movie is the worst movie ever made, I get to work with this elephant for three or four months. I'm definitely doing it."'

In a separate interview he joked with MTV that he decided to do the movie because of the name of his character, revealing: 'I just wanted to show I can be Jacob too. That's the only reason I did the movie. I just looked at the name. There was an elephant, my name is Jacob – done… The next movie I'm doing, I'm called Taylor in it.'

He added: 'I wasn't nervous at all until I started doing interviews for it and I realised I actually did a movie… It was just really fun while I was doing it. And now I remembered I actually made a movie. I think it's going to be great. It's really beautiful. It was really fun making it, so hopefully it will reflect in the movie.'

Water for Elephants received a score of 7.0 out of 10 from IMDb, based on 85,518 reviews. Critic Peter Travers awarded the movie 2.5 out of 4 stars in his review for *Rolling Stone*, writing: 'Sara Gruen's 2006 bestseller about forbidden love in the heated atmosphere of a Depression-era circus seemed a natural for the screen. And director Francis Lawrence (*I Am Legend*) and screenwriter Richard LaGravenese (*The Fisher King*) keep it carefully tended. So do its three stars. It's good to see Robert Pattinson, *Twilight*'s pale vampire prince, with color in his cheeks in the role of Jacob Jankowski, a Cornell student in veterinary medicine about to take his final exams when his parents die in a car crash.'

Rob is a huge animal lover and adopted a five-week-old puppy with Kristen from a rescue centre, just one day before he was due to be euthanised. Rob explained to chat-show host Ellen DeGeneres how he saved Bear, saying, 'He was in a five-day kill shelter and it was his fourth day. A couple of days [after adopting him], just by coincidence, I had to go back to LA and we had a private plane. So I took [Bear] from the worst pound in Monroe, Louisiana and he was sitting on a private jet the next day. We were staying at the Four Seasons afterwards. He didn't have any dog food so I got him a little plate of prosciutto.'

Because Bear was a mixed breed Rob had no idea how big he would grow but he thought he would end up being a big dog, but 'he just kind of got stunted.'

Rob and Kristen would later on end up adopting another mixed-breed dog, who they named Bernie. Kristen told on *Live! With Kelly and Michael*: 'They're really very different. I feel like I've raised Bear, whereas Bernie, we got her when she was like four, five – we're not positive – but she feels like my roommate. She's just like living in my house.'

Rob's next project was *Cosmopolis*, a movie written, directed and produced by David Cronenberg. Not the easiest director to work with by any stretch of the imagination, Cronenberg was once described by *The Village Voice* as 'the most audacious and challenging narrative director in the English-speaking world.' He was someone Rob had been dreaming of working with for a long time.

Rob was playing his lead character Eric Packer, a billionaire asset manager going about one day of his life, when everything he's involved with starts to unravel. Eric dresses well, he's comfortable with his excessive wealth and he's good at what he does. It was based on the 2003 novel of the same name by author Don DeLillo. Cronenberg didn't care about the *Twilight* movies or anything Rob had done before because he felt it didn't have any relevance to what they were filming but he did acknowledge that having Rob on the cast helped him to get the movie financed.

Once the cameras started rolling Cronenberg was impressed with how capable Rob was, telling *ETonline* on the DVD's release: 'He surprised me every day with good stuff. I don't do rehearsals, and I try not to shape the actor's performance at first. I want to see what his intuition is going to deliver. And then if there's a problem then I start to shape it, nudge it, manipulate it a little bit. I did very little of that with Rob.'

Cronenberg had wanted a lead who had charisma and had what it took to be in every scene and he definitely got that with Rob. He wanted to include a scene where Eric gets examined by a doctor in his limo and is told that he has an 'asymmetrical prostate' but that wasn't a problem for Rob, who understood that Cronenberg movies nearly always contain a theme of anal fixation.

The director and producer explained to *Yahoo Movies*: 'Orifices are the entry and exit of our bodies, and that really talks about identity and where the boundaries of an individual identity end and where the environment begins... I could do an academic analysis of my own movies, but that wouldn't help me create [my new] movies. ... You could do that analysis and make those connections amongst the movies, and you'd be correct.'

Not long after filming finished, it was time to start promoting *Breaking Dawn – Part 1* before it was released in cinemas on 18 November 2011. *Breaking Dawn – Part 1* received a score of 4.9 out of 10 from IMDb, based on 159,495 reviews. *Rolling Stone* labelled it the worst *Twilight* movie to date in their review, claiming: 'The picture is actually hurt by having a good director – *Gods and Monsters* and *Dream Girls* filmmaker Bill Condon – who focuses the camera on the faces of the actors, who are all far too blank and seem helpless in close-ups. Taylor Lautner is the worst of the bunch, often looking less like a sexy werewolf and more "like a petulant five-year-old."'

The Hollywood Reporter reviewer Todd McCarthy wrote: 'After the energy and alertness evident in his previous work as helmer of *Gods and Monsters*, *Kinsey* and *Dreamgirls*, it looks as though director Bill Condon fell into a trance while making this film – so dirgelike is the pacing, so banal is Melissa

Rosenberg's dutiful script on a scene-by-scene, moment-to-moment basis. It truly feels that 40 minutes or so, not two hours, would have been plenty to convey all that's necessary in the material covered.

'In the end, given how little goes on in *Breaking Dawn – Part 1* despite the major plot points, what you're left with is to gaze at the three leads, all of whom have their constituencies and reasons for being eminently watchable. The only hope is they'll have more to do next time around.'

The *Guardian*'s reviewer Peter Bradshaw only felt able to give it 1 star out of 5.

It was during interviews for the movie that Kristen finally confirmed that she was dating Rob, telling *GQ* that her 'boyfriend is English' and when asked for his name she replied: 'Come on, guys, it's so obvious!'

CHAPTER 15

HEARTBROKEN

It was in the year 2012 that Rob felt he was starting to be taken seriously as an actor but it was also the year his heart was broken.

He finally got to see *Bel Ami* in cinemas, two years after he'd filmed it. It had its world premiere at the 62nd Berlin International Film Festival before being released in limited cinemas on 8 June. It failed to make much of an impact, taking a measly $8,303,261 at the box office, and received a score of 5.4 out of 10 from IMDb, based on 14,100 reviews.

Movie critic Roger Ebert wasn't very flattering of Rob in his review, writing: 'Pattinson, alas, is an actor who hasn't mastered the art of smiling convincingly. He smiles as if saying "cheese!" In this world of sophisticated decadence, he needs a sardonic smile.'

Later on in his review he adds: 'The actresses do what they can with this sad sack. The surprise for me is Christina Ricci, who I think of as undernourished and nervous, but who flowers here in warm ripeness. Her character makes the mistake of actually loving Georges. This involves pure acting skill on her part, since Pattinson gives her so little to work with.'

San Francisco Gate reviewer Mike LaSalle was much more complimentary of Rob in his review: 'With his transparent thoughts and his odd way of moving his lips before any sound comes out of them, Pattinson is an idiosyncratic leading man, two parts James Dean to one part Tony Perkins. It's a pleasure to watch him onscreen and wait for the explosion.'

Rob had enjoyed filming the picture but had become a much better actor in the two years that had passed since the movie was filmed so he probably wasn't too upset by the negative reviews.

In May, *Cosmopolis* was first shown at the Cannes Film Festival, which meant a huge deal to Rob. The movie didn't receive any Oscar nominations but that didn't bother its director, Cronenberg. It did come second in *Cahiers du Cinema* top ten movies of 2012 and number 8 in *Sight & Sound*'s list, however, after its cinematic release in August.

Rob expressed to *Madame le Figaro* magazine how groundbreaking *Cosmopolis* had been for him (translated from French): '*Cosmopolis* is the movie of my life. I didn't consider myself an actor before, even if I had 10 years of acting behind me. I always felt like a fraud, and inappropriate. I doubted a lot. David Cronenberg gave me confidence in myself. He changed my way of acting and thinking in this industry.'

When the movie was praised by critics at the Cannes Film Festival Rob was overwhelmed. He confessed: 'Americans don't really know about Cannes or maybe they don't care, but for an English guy like me, it's so essential. As a kid, I would daydream in front of the pictures of the event and I collected the DVDs of the movies awarded. At Cannes, everything felt right because I was recognised by my peers.'

Kristen was there supporting him and was bursting with pride when she told MTV: 'He's so good in it! He's really, really [good]. I don't even know how he [did it]. I couldn't even understand it. It's so good, it's so cool, I'm so proud of him.'

Cosmopolis received a score of 5.0 out of 10 from IMDb, based on 33,609 reviews. *Variety*'s Justin Chang was full of praise in his review, writing: 'While commercial reach will be limited to the more adventurous end of the specialty market, Robert Pattinson's excellent performance reps an indispensable asset.'

The *Telegraph*'s Robbie Collin was equally impressed: 'At its heart is a sensational central performance from Robert Pattinson – yes, that Robert Pattinson – as Packer. Pattinson plays him like a human caldera; stony on the surface, with volcanic chambers of nervous energy and self-loathing churning deep below.'

ROBERT PATTINSON

Entertainment Weekly's Owen Gleiberman, full of admiration, wrote in his review: 'Robert Pattinson, pale and predatory even without his pasty-white vampire make-up, delivers his frigid *pensées* with rhythmic confidence, but he's not playing a character, he's playing an abstraction – the dapper gazillionaire hotshot who flies too close to the sun, but he likes it up there, so *f–* you! In the last act, he finally has a meeting with a man he can't control, the one who may be trying to kill him – played, with the only semblance of human spontaneity in the movie, by Paul Giamatti. But who cares what happens? Cronenberg has already murdered his protagonist. Or, at least, he has killed off any shred of life in him from the inside.'

Rob was so passionate about *Cosmopolis* that he became very defensive when people gave negative reviews, telling *The Vent*: 'I think *Cosmopolis* is really underrated; I think that's a great movie (laughs). I loved it. I'd do anything with [David Cronenberg]. I remember with *Cosmopolis*, when it came out, it's the first time I'd really been in a movie where if someone said they didn't like it, it was because they're an idiot (laughs). I felt very strongly about it.'

When *Blackbook* magazine interviewed Rob in July he confirmed that he and Kristen had no plans to get married yet, despite a gossip magazine claiming they were already making plans. He said: 'There was a magazine, with these pictures, saying I was getting married. No one ever knows what is true or what isn't. Even my own mum called to ask me if it was true. It's not. At least, not yet.'

Rob went from feeling extremely happy to extremely low when photographs of Kristen kissing Rupert Sanders, the married director of *Snow White and the Huntsman*, were published in July. They had been kissing in a car park and then drove to a hiking trail for more kissing.

The secret rendezvous had taken place on 17 July, but the photos weren't published for a few days. On 18 July, Rob had been seen with Kristen at Hotel Café enjoying listening to some music and then on 22 July they went to the Teen Choice Awards together and picked up an award for *Breaking Dawn – Part 1*.

The news broke on 24 July and the next day Kristen released a statement through *People* magazine. In it she said: 'I'm deeply sorry for the hurt and embarrassment I've caused to those close to me and everyone this has affected. This momentary indiscretion has jeopardised the most important thing in my life, the person I love and respect the most, Rob. I love him, I love him, I'm so sorry.'

But the affair didn't just affect Rob. Rupert's wife, English model and actress Liberty Ross, was absolutely devastated and tweeted 'Wow' before deleting her account. She was upset not just for herself but for the couple's two children too.

From then on Rob and Kristen's relationship status became front-page news and it was extremely difficult for him to take in because he felt so betrayed and everything was so public.

The agony of having everything played out in the media left Rob wanting to say very little about his personal life in future interviews. He didn't want to give the gossip journalists anything they could twist into a story to sell magazines so he kept his head down and hoped things would calm down.

Removal trucks were spotted outside the home he shared with Kristen in the Los Feliz neighbourhood of San Francisco on 29 July (he had bought it in September 2011 for $6.2 million) but then things went quiet, with the media wondering where Rob had disappeared to until he was spotted out with friends at a place called the Deer Lodge. Workwise, he wasn't due to film any more movies in 2012, but he signed up for lots of exciting projects that would be filmed in 2013.

Kristen had been supposed to present with Rob at the MTV Video Music Awards in September but she'd pulled out. However, when interviewed at the Toronto Film Festival she'd hinted that they were giving it another go, 'We're going to be fine. We're totally fine,' she told one reporter.

By the end of the month it was reported that they'd moved back in with each other. They managed to escape the glare of the paparazzi for a few weeks but were then photographed at a bar together on 16 October. Three days later, photos of Kristen and Rob kissing by the pool of her new home were published.

By the time Rob was standing on the black carpet at the *Breaking Dawn – Part 2* World premiere in Los Angeles he felt relieved that the *Twilight Saga* had come to an end.

Twilight had taken over his life for five years; he had loved it but now he was ready for the next chapter in his career. He had finished filming in April 2011 so it felt like a lifetime ago. Fans thought he seemed relaxed on the black carpet and seemed totally at ease with Kristen too. Both Rob and Kristen refused to talk about their private lives but they were happy to talk about the movie.

Rob confessed to *E! Online*: 'In a year, I think I'll definitely miss it. It's such a strange experience. That's why I waited to see the movie until tonight. It's such a different thing seeing it with the fans instead of on a DVD or whatever.'

His favourite moments of the whole *Saga* were filming the scene where Edward and Bella are dancing and looking up at the stars and the scene in Brazil where things got out of control. *Twilight* fans had been hired as extras and they went crazy until they saw Rob and Kristen – there was a mini riot and three cameras got broken in the stampede.

For the premiere Rob decided to wear a green-and-black Gucci suit with a pale grey shirt and black tie. Originally he had planned to team the suit with a red shirt until his manager accused him of looking like a Christmas tree. Rob had actually had a hand in designing the suit with the team at Gucci, which no doubt made it extra-special. He'd picked green because he'd had a dream where he was wearing an emerald green houndstooth suit and it had looked great!

> **DID YOU KNOW?**
>
> They actually filmed all the movies within the space of two years so for Rob it kind of felt like one massive movie at times, not five individual ones.

Thousands of fans had turned up to see the cast enjoy their final *Twilight Saga* premiere on Monday, 12 November 2012. Some had been camping for days in order to secure good spots close to the barriers. Rob hoped they would continue to support him when he moved on to other movies but even if they didn't, it didn't worry him too much.

It was nice to be among Ashley Greene, Nikki Reed, Jackson Rathbone and the rest of the cast again. They hadn't all been together for a year at least, as filming for the movie had wrapped for most of the cast on 15 April 2011. They'd done a small amount of re-shoots in April 2012, but not everyone had been involved. Rob felt that it was a shame no one had organised a party and that they couldn't all go out for a drink or celebrate because they had to fly out to England straight afterwards for the London premiere.

Breaking Dawn – Part 2 received a score of 5.6 out of 10 from IMDb, based on 157,563 reviews.

It received better reviews than *Breaking Dawn – Part 1*, although critics were still rather negative about it. *The New York Times*'s Manohla Dargis titled his review 'Infusing the

Bloodline with a Problem Child' and wrote: 'The glammed up Ms. Stewart, hair flowing and jaw squared, finally looks like the star she has become over the course of the series. Alas, she also acts kind of dead. Apparently becoming a vampire robs you of the power to put across an emotion persuasively, and while Bella looks lovely or at least strikingly styled, she's also pretty much a stiff. Mr. Pattinson, by contrast, has rarely appeared more relaxed, and his character has never seemed more, well, human. You have a lot of time to look at their faces, to examine their micro-movements, the cut of their clothes, the curl of their hair – and also idly to wonder what was going on between these two tabloid favorites during production – because, beyond a quick hunt and an alfresco nosh, not much happens during the initial, narratively thin stretch.'

Empire's Helen O'Hara finished her review by stating: 'Fans will be left on a high; other viewers will be confused but generally entertained by a saga whose romance is matched only by its weirdness.'

New York Post's Sara Stewart echoed this sentiment, writing in her review: 'It wouldn't be fair to go into much detail about the way things shake out, but suffice to say Italian baddies like brother and sister Jane and Alec (Dakota Fanning and Cameron Bright) are given the sort of treatment fans will likely be cheering for, and Condon departs enough from the plot of the book that Twihards will have a few surprises in store rather than just waiting to hear all the relevant lines doled out.

'They'll still be a little sad to see this silly series wrap up, as am I. Over the past four years this much-maligned franchise has certainly descended to B-movie lows, but it's also been partly responsible for spawning one of the fastest-growing movie demographics out there: the rabid fangirl. And she's only going to get hungrier.'

Rob ended 2012 surrounded by those he loved. He flew back to the UK to spend time with his family over Christmas, with Kristen staying behind in LA. The media reported that she hadn't joined him because his sisters hadn't forgiven her for cheating on him with Rupert Sanders and this might have caused awkwardness around the dining table. Rob and Kristen didn't respond to any of the reports, deciding to keep their decision to celebrate Christmas separately a secret.

However, Rob had earlier told a reporter that on a typical Christmas he has an argument with every member of his family and falls asleep on the sofa by three o'clock. He loves how this happens every year.

Despite spending Christmas apart the couple did spend New Year together after Kristen flew to London. They enjoyed a romantic meal at a Mexican restaurant called Mestizo and posed for a photo with the staff waiting on them. Neither of them dressed up for the occasion, which in a way made them stand out from the rest of the diners, who were dressed up, ready to ring in 2013.

CHAPTER 16
PUSHING HIMSELF

Rob had a busy year planned for 2013. He had been asked to present at the 70th Golden Globe Awards on Sunday, 13 January at the International Ballroom of the Beverly Hilton, in Beverly Hills, California. This was a great honour and would see him reunited with Amanda Seyfried, with whom he had presented at the 2009 Oscars.

Their category was Screenplay Motion Picture and after Amanda introduced the category it was down to Rob to announce the winner, Quentin Tarantino.

Only a few days after the ceremony he had to pack his bags and catch a flight to Australia, as principal photography for his new movie *The Rover* was starting on 28 January. He was to spend seven weeks filming in various parts of the country alongside Guy Pearce, Scoot McNairy and Gillian Jones.

The movie was set in the Australian outback, ten years after a global economic collapse. In that time Australia had become similar to a third-world country. Rob was to play the part of Rey, a naive young American man who is abandoned by his brother when a robbery goes wrong and ends up being taken under the wing of a violent and brutal former soldier who is out for revenge.

When Rob had first been sent the script by his agent it had immediately caught his eye because of the way it had been laid out on the page. There wasn't as much dialogue as one would expect from a movie script and there was a lack of punctuation. It offered so much freedom. Initially, he thought that he was being offered the part without having to audition but alas, his agent informed him that lots of actors were after the same role so he would have to put in an amazing audition in order to secure the part.

His audition for director David Michôd had lasted for four hours and he was really put through his paces. Michôd had never seen *Twilight* or any of Rob's other movies so he was judging him purely on the audition. He wanted to see exactly how Rob would play Rey if he won the part, how he would move, how he would convey Rey's slowness and his neediness.

Michôd had found watching Rob captivating, he liked how clever he was and how passionate he was about working with directors he admired. He knew he didn't have to keep searching, he had found the right man for the job. He told *The Hollywood*

Reporter: 'He came through with flying colours. He came the closest of any actor to walking into the room with a beautiful, fully realised version of the character that was not dissimilar to mine. It was exhilarating because I could suddenly see the movie.'

Rob found that as soon as he put on Rey's clothes, his jeans, his T-shirts and oversized sneakers that he somehow became Rey; he walked differently, his mannerisms changed. He had to look unkempt and unshaven. Rey came from a different world, a harsher background, where staying alive was all that mattered.

When asked by BBC America how he would describe his character, Rob said: 'I think he's someone who's basically been severely bullied by everyone… he's been convinced by his family and whoever he grew up with that he's in some way slow and mentally deficient. But I don't actually think he is, he's just been told it so many times that he's just regressed inside himself. He thinks he's incapable of thought, he just wants to be told what to do all the time.'

DID YOU KNOW?
Rob thought that Rey was the most interesting character he had ever played.

Rob enjoyed not having to look beautiful and pristine, telling *The Vent*: 'It takes away constraints. If someone's saying, "You've got to look pretty!" for one thing you feel like a bit of an idiot, because you're a guy, and then you're kind of thinking about stuff that really doesn't mean anything – you're just posing. As soon as you take away the allowance for your own vanity, then it's kind of a relief.'

They asked him how he would describe the themes of *The Rover* and he replied: 'I think it's just a story about survivors. I think they're quite simple people in extraordinary circumstances. They're trying to figure out how to live when it seems like there's not a lot of hope. It seems like there's nothing to do tomorrow, so what are you supposed to do at any point during your day? Even the gang I'm in, they're stealing money and there's nothing to use the money for at all (laughs). Eric [Guy Pearce] says, "It's worthless, it's just paper." It's very difficult to know why [you need] to keep living if everything seems totally worthless, and yet people do.'

Cynthia Parker from *TheWrap* was interested in how Rob developed Rey's accent. He confessed: 'I'm not entirely sure… I had this one tape of this guy from Florida, from St Petersburg, Florida. I liked his kind of… fun accent. I kinda took little bits from that… a bit from Kentucky as well.'

When she pointed out that Rey's accent was very different from his brother's, Rob couldn't help but laugh. 'That's Scoot's fault!' he replied. [Scoot McNairy played Henry, Rey's brother.]

The final two weeks of the shoot took place in a remote town called Marree, 685 kilometres north of Adelaide. The town's ninety or so residents loved having the cast and crew among them. While he was in the town Rob was interviewed by the *Daily Telegraph*. They wondered how he had managed to cope with the heat, day-in, day-out, but he saw the discomfort he felt had helped him perform. He told them: 'It's added lots to the performance – being covered in dirt, pouring sweat, with tons of flies around. You lose your inhibitions quite quickly.

'You definitely end up making a different movie [filming in the outback as opposed to filming in Hollywood]. Being in the desert has a funny effect. It does change you in a way.'

DID YOU KNOW?
There were so many flies that it really put Rob off eating because they were all over the crew's food. He admitted to *ET* that he resorted to just eating bread with barbecue sauce, saying, 'I ate that every single day, every meal for about three weeks.' When he got back to civilisation he went to a restaurant and ordered lots of vegetable sides, explaining that, 'I was just eating bowls of broccoli.'

Aside from the flies and the unbearable heat, Rob thoroughly enjoyed working on *The Rover*. The whole cast and crew really bonded and would stay up late drinking and talking. Rob told *The Vent*: 'It was amazing, because the whole crew was staying in the same place and there was nothing else to do, we were living in a pub. It's annoying if you're in an unfamiliar city and all the people you work with are from that city, they all go home, so you're just stuck in your hotel.

'When you can hang out with a bunch of new people, you get close to them really quickly, especially when there's literally nothing else to do. It's really fun. I hadn't done that for a long time. I had a fantastic experience making this film.'

When a journalist from *The Courier Mail* asked how being in a different time zone and not having phone signal had affected his private life while filming *The Rover* in Australia, Rob had confessed: 'Yeah, it's tough. But at the end of the day, it's only two months.'

Once they wrapped, he returned to Los Angeles and gave himself a well-deserved three weeks off. A while later, Rob was given the opportunity to do something he'd never done before. Although his face had been on literally hundreds of different T-shirts, mugs, pyjamas, bedding, bags… and endless other items, thanks to *Twilight*, he had never actually accepted the opportunity of endorsing a brand, until he was approached by Dior.

They wanted Rob to be the face of their new Dior Homme campaign, taking over from Jude Law. After discussing exactly what they would require him to do, he agreed, as long as he was given creative control. He wasn't about to do something that he didn't feel comfortable with, just to make money and Dior had had to prove that they were the right brand to get his backing.

The advert was entitled 'The Film', telling the story of a young couple in New York. Directed by Romain Gavras, it was set to the music track 'Whole Lotta Love' by Led Zeppelin. Rob handpicked Gavras for the job, as he loved how controversial his work was: he had directed the video for M.I.A.'s track 'Born Free' in 2010, which had been banned because of its graphic content.

Together they tried to create something that was different from a typical fragrance ad. Rob's character didn't drive a flash car or seem overly wealthy and the relationship with his love interest (played by French model Camille Rowe) was shown as being somewhat self-destructive.

They chose to shoot in black-and-white to give the film a timeless quality, and cut Rob's hair shorter than he normally has it. For the scene where Rob drives a convertible BMW on the beach they had to shoot at 7am. 'The sand was wet, the car was getting stuck in it,' he told French magazine *Premiere*. 'So, I had to drive at 100 km/h with the two models in the back while Romain was screaming: "We're losing the light! We're losing the light!" I never thought I'd ever find myself in that kind of ad, but I have to admit that it was a really positive experience. Dior gave us a very incredulous amount of freedom.'

Rob was pleased with what they achieved; he liked how someone watching wouldn't necessarily know it was a fragrance ad until right at the last second when the bottle appears and the voice-over says 'Dior Homme'. For some time he had wanted to work with Gavras, in fact, he'd become quite obsessed by the idea, so to have managed to get him to direct the advert had been hugely satisfying.

DID YOU KNOW?

The first fragrance Rob ever wore was L'Eau d'Issey. It had been a gift from his aunt when he was twelve. When he wore it, it made him feel invisible and he credited smelling of cologne with getting him into bars when he was on holiday. He always remembers his dad wearing Brut by Fabergé when he was growing up, but the smell he most associates with his mum is not perfume, but potpourri because she used to be obsessed with it when he was younger.

For the press launch Rob was dressed in a Dior suit and black turtleneck, but for the one-on-one media interviews the next day he was back to his normal style – white T-shirt, grey hoodie, jeans and a baseball cap. He wasn't going to pretend to be something he's not; having the freedom to dress as he wishes really matters to him. Like any big star, he does have a stylist (otherwise how would he find time to shop for clothes when his schedule is so packed?), but rather than dictate what he should wear, Rob's stylist lets him choose from a range. Wearing clothes he feels comfortable in is always important, especially on his rare days off.

Rob admitted in interviews that house hunting was high on his agenda. He'd been looking at properties online and in person whenever he got the chance, as he was renting in Beverly Hills and wanted his own place again. He was excited about doing more movies, and wasn't planning any holidays, even though he hadn't been on vacation for many years. He didn't consider himself a workaholic and didn't feel like he needed to take time out because he wasn't feeling particularly tired.

His mantra was driven by fear in some respects; he wanted to keep getting better at acting, to keep trying new things because this would open up new avenues for him. He'd grown up wanting to be like his dad: masculine, wise and strong, and had achieved that. He felt that if he stopped striving for things then he would waste the opportunities he had already been given.

When *The Vent* asked him what his hobbies were he laughed and said: 'When I'm not working, I try to get another job, constantly. You start to realise there's a finite amount of time to get stuff done, and there's a lot of different things that I want to achieve, also I like working pretty much more than anything else in my life. My job is my hobby.'

But he did admit, 'I just started [writing songs] again recently. I generally just do stuff that sounds nice. I don't really write songs in a conventional way. I don't write lyrics separately, it's quite instinctive.'

While promoting Dior Homme he was asked by one journalist from *Grazia.es* what London, New York and Paris smell like. It was a pretty strange question but Rob answered it intelligently. He said (translated): 'What I miss the most about London, aside from my family and friends, is the smell of rain. Both Heathrow and Gatwick are surrounded by fields and when you land you can smell wet grass. New York is completely different. To me, it smells like food, there's lots of it everywhere. And Paris is a different world. More than a scent, I associate it with something more visual. It's pure energy. I love getting lost in its streets.'

In April, Rob didn't visit Kristen on her birthday, which made fans think that their relationship was well and truly over. They felt that Rob had always been a considerate boyfriend and if they had still been together then he definitely would have made the trip. The previous year, Rob had gone with Kristen to the Coachella Valley Music and Arts Festival and they'd had a crazy time, listening to the bands performing and partying. He decided to still attend the festival but instead of going with Kristen, he went with 'Roar' singer Katy Perry. He was later spotted moving suitcases and belongings out of Kristen's home on 23 May.

In the weeks that followed Rob and Katy met up a few times but she was just being a good friend to him, they weren't about to start a relationship. But the media did what they do best and blew the whole thing out of proportion.

Katy decided to set the record straight during an interview with *Elle* magazine, using her own unique sense of humour. She told the magazine: 'OK, so here's the proof there was never anything going on with me and Robert Pattinson. I fart in front of him. Properly fart. And I never, ever fart in front of a man I am dating. That's a rule.

'He's my bud. I'm like his big sister. We just hang out. The other day, I said: "One of the things I'm most proud of is not sleeping with you, Robert." And that's true.'

She also admitted she'd contacted Kristen directly to make sure that she understood that nothing was going on between them, explaining, 'I sent her a text message saying: "I know you've seen all this stuff, but you know I would never disrespect you. I'm not that person. I'm just trying to be a friend to him but it is unfortunate that I do have a set of tits."'

August saw Rob focus on acting again as he was shooting *Maps to the Stars* in Toronto and Los Angeles. He had decided to do challenging movies like *The Rover* and *Maps to the Stars*, 'because I feel like I've done quite a few things where I'm quite still. I'm trying to find people that are doing things that feel dangerous,' he told *Reuters* at the time.

And he wanted to be best known for his acting ability again, not for the fact that Kristen Stewart had cheated on him. He felt that all of his twenties up until this point he'd been playing Edward and in many ways he was at a crossroads. He hadn't felt like an adult until his twenty-sixth birthday so he thought it was the perfect time to leave the *Twilight Saga* and move on.

While he had been doing the promotional tour for the final movie he hadn't been able to contain his excitement for his future films, telling a journalist from *Empire*: 'I'm trying to recreate my DVD shelf from when I was seventeen, I'm just working with every director... David Michôd, I literally had the DVD... *Animal Kingdom* is one of the best movies of the last five years. I'm really excited to be working with him [on *The Rover*]. That group that they were part of in Australia, Blue Tongue Films... Joel Edgerton, Nash his brother... they were all friends and now they've basically become the coolest thing in the Australian film industry.

'I'm working with James Marsh who did *Man on Wire* and *Project Nim* in a movie with Carey Mulligan [sadly the movie was later put on hold because of scheduling conflicts]. I'm doing another movie with Cronenberg...'

Rob's love of cinema, and in particular his knowledge of French directors, really impressed David Cronenburg when they started working together on *Cosmopolis*. The director told *First Post.com*: '[Rob] is very knowledgeable about cinema... I don't think his *Twilight* fans realise this about him, but he's really an aficionado about art cinema. I mean, on the set I'd find him talking to Juliette Binoche about obscure French cinema, (chuckles) so you know, he brings a real depth of understanding of the history and art of cinema and all of those things mean that you have a lot of power and a lot of responsiveness from your actor as a director. It's like driving the Ferrari instead of driving, you know, a Volkwagen Beetle. And you get that with Rob. I must also add, he's very down to earth and very easy to work with. He's not a diva at all, you know. He's really a sweetheart.'

Rob really admires the work of French director Jean-Luc Godard so having the opportunity to chat to Juliette Binoche and David Cronenburg about his movies must have been very refreshing. He shared with *Rotten Tomatoes* how much he loves Godard's movie *Prénom Carmen* (1983), saying, 'It's actually one of my favourite films. I think it's the best Godard film – it's like his version of *Carmen* the opera, one of his films from the eighties. In terms of just pure film-making and manipulating an audience, it kind of starts out as a farce, as a complete, stupid farce, with this bank robbery but it's really, really Godardian, with kind of a stupid humour that's so random. Only he could make it, mixed up with these kinds of philosophical elements.'

Rob also rates French actor Romain Duris, who played gangster Thomas Seyr in *The Beat That My Heart Skipped* (2005) and bumbling novelist Xavier in *Russian Dolls* (2005). He loves how versatile he is, how he can take on parts that are the polar opposite of each other and do them both so well. Watching actors like Duris do this makes Rob want to do the same.

Other actors who have influenced Rob include Jack Nicholson, his childhood hero. He grew up watching his movies, and has seen every single one of them, from his first movie, *The Cry Baby Killer* (1958), to his last, *How Do You Know* (2010).

Rob told the *Daily Mirror*: 'My favourite actor is Jack Nicholson. I watched *One Flew Over The Cuckoo's Nest* when I was about thirteen and I used to try and be him in virtually everything I did. I dressed like him, I tried to do his accent – I think it kind of stuck with me.'

Taking on the persona of Nicholson's character Randle McMurphy from *One Flew Over The Cuckoo's Nest* helped Rob become more confident and outspoken as a teenager. He still feels Nicholson influences him today and told *Swiss Faces* magazine when they asked who his fashion inspiration is: 'I've always admired people who dressed practically. I somehow think that's especially manly. I like clothes that last for a long time; until all that is left is the material they were made of. I'm thinking about Jack Nicholson's clothes in *The Shining* or *One Flew over the Cuckoo's Nest*; actually pretty much everything he's worn in these films.'

Rob also loved watching James Dean movies when he was growing up, and the way Dean spoke and acted was something that he tried to emulate. He told the *Daily Mirror* in 2008: 'I always say I've stolen things from James Dean's voice, the way he slurs his words, just for chatting up girls and stuff.'

He found watching Dean's movie *Rebel Without a Cause* (1955) really helped him prepare to play Edward Cullen for the first time. 'It influenced the hair and stuff. In lots of ways, it has a very similar character arc – an everyday girl brings this relatively strange individual out of his slump,' he admitted to the *New York Daily News*.

Rob wasn't just a fan of *Rebel Without a Cause*, he enjoyed watching Dean's other movies *East of Eden* (1955) and *Giant* (1956) too. Tragically, Dean died in a car crash when he was only twenty-four so he never had the opportunity to make any more films.

When Rob finds a movie he loves he isn't afraid to watch it over and over again, as he finds he enjoys it on every occasion, even when he knows all the lines and exactly what will happen in each scene. One of his favourite movies of all time is the Bernard Rose directed *Ivansxtc*, which was released in 2002 and was based on the Leo Tolstoy novel, *The Death of Ivan Ilyich*. Rob ended up watching the movie more than fifty times in 2008 alone. He really rates the lead actor Danny Huston, who has been in lots of mainstream movies including *The Constant Gardener* (2005), *X-Men Origins: Wolverine* (2009), *Clash of the Titans* (2010) and *Robin Hood* (2010), but is perhaps best known for being the brother of actress Anjelica Huston.

Ivansxtc tells the tale of Ivan Beckman, a Hollywood talent agent (played by Huston), who dies suddenly. His associates and 'friends' think he has died of a drugs overdose but in fact he was suffering from cancer and had spent his last few days trying to tell them and sorting out his affairs. It's a movie about fame, power, sex and drugs and as such was awarded an 18-certificate rating.

For David Cronenberg, working with Rob on *Cosmopolis* had been an absolute pleasure, so offering him the part of Jerome Fontana in *Maps to the Stars* was an easy decision to make. 'I really think he's a terrific actor. He's extremely inventive. He surprised me every day on *Cosmopolis* with the nuances and things that he did which were unexpected. Of course I was very familiar with the dialogue and yet he would surprise me,' Cronenberg revealed to *The Playlist*, 'and I thought, this is a guy who I would like to work with some more, which is how I felt with Viggo Mortensen. When you find an actor who surprises you every day, you figure he could do it some more with a completely different role in a completely different movie.'

Rob was thrilled to have the opportunity to work with Cronenberg again, and told Mike Hogan from *Vanity Fair*: '[I was so excited] I hadn't even read the script and I was like, "Yep." That was another character who didn't have any kind of back story or anything. I said, "What kind of guy do you think he is?" And he said, "I don't know, what do you think?" And we are shooting in two days and I'm like, Great. It's exactly what happened on *Cosmopolis*. We don't talk about it at all and then turn up and every single scene I did was one take. It's ridiculous.

'With *Cosmopolis*, he knew exactly what he wanted. With *Maps*, he just liked what I was doing on the first take.'

Maps to the Stars is a movie that explores the twisted side of Hollywood, with every character aside from Rob's seeming to go insane by the end. David Cronenberg had chosen some big names to be in the cast. Julianne Moore, John Cusack and Mia Wasikowska had never worked with Rob before but they were all excited to work on the project with him.

Rob was playing a young limo driver called Jerome, who also acts and dreams of being a screenwriter. During the course of the movie he has a relationship with Agatha [played by Mia Wasikowska] and sleeps with Havana [Julianne Moore].

In fact, Rob believes the movie is about people who lie to themselves – right up until the end, explaining: 'I don't really think it's taking the piss out of Hollywood. It's very specific [to these characters]. I think Benjie is probably the truest character. I've met a lot of [child star] kids like him. The scene with him and the little girls bitching about everybody – you just see that a lot. When you see these kids, there is only one way: you either get in therapy now or become a serial killer, or kill yourself. I mean, you can see it really early on – it's terrifying.'

Even though Rob had a taste of fame when he was seventeen by playing Cedric Diggory in *Harry Potter* he didn't play Edward in *Twilight* for another four years, so he had a chance of experiencing normal life. He thinks living in London from the age of eighteen to twenty-one really helped shape who he is as a person, and thinks it's a real shame child actors don't get the chance to have a normal life. It's hard enough for him when he auditions for a part and then doesn't get it, so for a child of eight or ten it must be ten times worse.

Cronenberg felt that fans of Bruce Wagner, who had written the screenplay and novel, would instantly be able to tell he was the movie's writer because 'it's sort of a condensed essence of Bruce. And while it's satirical, it's also very powerful, emotionally, and insightful and funny,' he divulged to *The Playlist*. Rob agreed, describing it as a 'cutting comedy, dark and seriously funny.'

While they were filming the movie Rob took time out to visit the Children's Hospital, Los Angeles. He wanted to give the young patients something to smile about so asked the staff if he could be a surprise guest. The second Rob entered the Teen Lounge the children couldn't believe it was really him; they couldn't believe 'Edward Cullen' had come to see them. Rob was delighted to see their smiling faces and joined in with various crafting activities that had been arranged. He had a go at decorating a photo frame but wasn't impressed with his artistry skills, although he thought the children's frames were great and signed the frames of those children who asked him to.

Before leaving, he made a special trip to the rooms of two cystic fibrosis patients who were huge *Twilight* fans but not well enough to leave their rooms.

Lyndsay Hutchison, who works at the hospital, told reporters: 'We couldn't help laughing and smiling when one of the patients was so star-struck that she couldn't speak. You could tell it meant the world to her – she was tearing up and smiling ear-to-ear as we were leaving. The other little girl teased him relentlessly and begged him to do an American accent. They were instant friends.'

Her colleague added: 'Robert was so nervous about meeting the kids – he didn't want to let them down – which is a testament to how humble he is. He was incredibly gracious and kind. He will probably never fully understand what a huge lift he gave to these kids today, and how it will positively impact them over the long term.'

Rob's respect for David Cronenberg was clear in virtually every interview he gave on the movie. He explained to one French journalist how he'd previously worked with some directors who had lost their direction during filming, but ever the professional, he didn't reveal the names of those he was referring to. He admired how passionate Cronenberg was about his work, even after being part of the movie industry for over forty years, and went so far as to say that he would like to be like Cronenberg one day.

Working on *Maps to the Stars* in a way confirmed to Rob

just how crazy Hollywood is and how he will never be able to fade into obscurity. He wishes there was no Internet, no Twitter and no gossip websites, but he knows they aren't going to disappear so he has to accept that his life will continue to be under scrutiny.

He absolutely hates the paparazzi and recalled to *The Hollywood Reporter* about one particular day when he tried to evade them because he didn't want them to find his new address. He said: 'It was like eight cars following me. And this went on for ten hours, this thing. I literally didn't know what to do. [But] you figure out ways to deal with it. It's been such a long time now, it just becomes what your life is. I can't even really remember what my life was like before.'

> ### DID YOU KNOW?
> When things get tough, Rob can always pick up the phone and speak to his manager, 3 Arts Entertainment's Nick Frenkel, and agent Stephenie Ritz. He really trusts them because they have been supporting him on a personal and professional level for many years.

Rob's fans were surprised when *E! Online* published photos of Kristen leaving his home after spending four hours with him on 30 October. Although the paparazzi didn't manage to capture Kristen and Rob together, they did capture Kristen driving her car away, and then Rob driving his car not far behind her. It was the first time they had been spotted together since May.

By December there had been no more public sightings of Rob and Kristen together so fans came to the conclusion that they had both decided that it was best to move on. Rob flew out to London for Christmas as usual, and thoroughly enjoyed catching up with his friends and family. He went to the same pub he likes to visit every Christmas Eve, wished fans a Merry Christmas and posed for photos. But he wasn't the only famous face in the pub – football commentator Adrian Chiles and celebrity chef Heston Blumenthal were there too.

After enjoying a quiet Christmas day with his family he was spotted having a drink with London-based artist Nettie Wakefield on Boxing Day. The press reported that they had been giggling and flirting in the pub and suggested that Nettie could be Rob's new girlfriend. They were so desperate to make out that Rob had moved on from Kristen. Poor Rob had only wanted to have a little catch-up with his friend before he had to fly back to America – but according to the press he wasn't allowed to have female friends.

Rather than fly back to Los Angeles Rob headed to New York as he was going to be ringing in 2014 with his good friend, model Jamie Strachan and his girlfriend Dakota Fanning. It was the first New Year's Eve he hadn't spent in the UK for many years.

A few days later he flew all the way back to London to have

more time with his family and was spotted having dinner with his sister and friends at the Mosob Eritrean Restaurant on 8 January. *Queen of the Desert* filming was due to start in Merzouga, Morocco, on 13 January, so Rob only had a few days in London. They would be filming in Marrakesh, the fourth biggest city in the world, in Arfoud, a town in the Sahara Desert, and Ouarzazate, nicknamed 'the door of the desert', which had been used as a location in *Lawrence of Arabia* (1962), *Gladiator* (2000), *Salmon Fishing in the Yemen* (2011) and many more movies.

Rob had only a small role in the movie, which meant that once he had shot his scenes he could leave and head to Toronto, Canada, to film another movie, *Life*. He explained to a journalist from the *Independent* about the character he plays in *Queen of the Desert*: 'It's sort of close to the real guy, it's certainly not Lawrence of Arabia-like. It's a small part as well… It's quite nice doing small parts. The film isn't totally reliant on what I do, so I get to work with who I want to work with and it's not my fault if it doesn't make any money.'

Filming for *Life* began on 18 February and finished on 27 March. Set in the 1950s, the movie was based on a true story. Rob was playing photographer Dennis Stock, who struck up a friendship with actor James Dean after he travelled with him through Los Angeles, New York and Indiana.

Dane DeHaan of *In Treatment* fame was to play James Dean, while Oscar-winning actor Ben Kingsley would play Jack

Warner, president of Warner Bros. Studios, and *Great Gatsby*'s Joel Edgerton was to play picture editor John G. Morris.

Filming in Toronto in winter was very challenging for Rob and the rest of the cast because they had to wear period costumes, which were very thin and offered hardly any protection from the freezing temperatures. The movie's director Anton Corbijn was impressed with how they coped and how the audience watching the movie would have no idea of the discomfort they had been in during the shoot because they didn't let it affect their performances.

As well as shooting in Toronto, they shot scenes in Los Angeles, taking over the legendary Chateau Marmont hotel and the Pantages Theatre. Rob told *The Vent*: 'It was fun to do... Anton[Corbijn]'s really cool. It's about the famous photographs of James Dean in Times Square; it's about James Dean and the photographer's relationship. Joel Edgerton's in it, weirdly because he's a co-writer on *The Rover*, and Ben Kingsley. It's cool. It's interesting doing a movie about photography with Anton Corbijn, a master photographer. He taught me how to take photos a little bit, with an old Leica. They're not very good. I thought they were all going to be absolutely amazing. I developed them all at the end of the movie and I did, like, twenty-five rolls of film, and on about four I hadn't even realised that you need to pull the lens out (laughs) – so they're all blank. Four films. It was a fun movie to do.'

Even though James Dean is one of Rob's idols he wasn't

interested in playing him in the movie, explaining, 'Dane [DeHaan] is so brave doing it. It's one of the hardest parts ever. Try and play any iconic person. Dane's got a wig, fake earlobes, and contact lenses – the whole deal. And James Dean's mannerisms are so recognisable, so you've got to play the part and all this other stuff. It's like playing Harry Potter – everyone's got expectations – whereas I'm just the observer.'

In May, Rob returned to the Cannes Film Festival to promote not just one film but two, *Maps to the Stars* and *The Rover*. Some of the journalists interviewing him mentioned how the year before he had been promoting *Cosmopolis* and both that movie and *Maps to the Stars* involved a limousine. Rob teased that he and David Cronenberg were perhaps building a limousine-themed trilogy.

French magazine *Premiere* wanted to talk to him about his sex scene with Julianne Moore in *Maps to the Stars* but this didn't bother Rob, as he has no qualms about sharing how awkward he finds it doing sex scenes with legendary actresses he has only just met. He revealed: 'I remember seeing Julianne before we started shooting the scene. She was giving me advice: "Keep choosing classy projects and filming intelligent films." And suddenly, David says "Action!" and we start f****** like beasts in the car. Very classy, that's right… (Laughing). On top of that, it was boiling hot. I was sweating like crazy and huge drops of sweat were running down my forehead. I asked myself if I wasn't having a heart attack. Every time a drop was falling,

I was trying to stop it from ending up on Julianne's back. It was ridiculous. After a while she turned back in my direction, worried, and asked me: "Are you okay? Are you having a panic attack?" I was out of breath, completely drenched, meanwhile her, not at all.'

Rob also got sweaty filming *The Rover*, revealing, 'It's my own sweat that you see on the screen. In *The Rover*, my problem was the flies. I had never seen anything like it. We were constantly covered in fake blood and once we came out, fifty flies started surrounding us. All day long, it wouldn't stop.

'We really shot the movie in the middle of nowhere. Most of the people you see in the movie were recruited on the same day, like this small guy who sells a gun to Guy Pearce and walks and grumbles: "F***, f***, f***!" He really was like that. There was also this guy with the crazy face we see in the shop. They found him while they were looking at the place. He came into the house thinking it was deserted and came face to face with this guy and his wife, who were naked – they found out later that she was a naturist.'

Rob is always passionate about his movies because he never takes on something that isn't going to challenge him in some way. He felt that he learnt a lot from filming *The Rover* and playing such a vulnerable character. The movie's director David Michôd wasn't a dictator and let Rob add personal touches to his character – so he decided to shave the back of his head to play Rey and have his teeth painted so they looked rotten. He explained to *Vanity Fair*: 'Initially it was [supposed to be that] they didn't have fluoride in the water so everyone's teeth were messed up, but then I end up being the only one with really messed-up teeth. I put it down to, he was just one of those kids who didn't brush his teeth. I think it's quite a distinct person, and I knew a few of them in school – kids who had brown teeth at eleven and were always, like, really weird.'

It was Rob's idea to give Ray a strange tattoo on his arm, as Michôd explained to fan site *Robert Pattinson Australia*: 'We had long conversations about things like tattoos and stuff, and what I started to glean for it after a while was that we were creating a character who in slightly different circumstances would be just a kid doing the things that kids do, having girlfriends, listening to their favourite music and getting stupid tattoos.'

DID YOU KNOW?

Fans thought the tattoo Rob chose depicted a sexual act but it was actually of a sculpture called *Femme au Bouquet* by artist Julien Dillens. Rob felt that the tattoo's design really suited his character so that's why he chose it.

Michôd liked to let his actors fill in the gaps in the script, he didn't provide them with a detailed document explaining the back story before they started shooting. When *Vanity Fair*

Above left: A fresh-faced Robert at a photo call for *Harry Potter and the Goblet of Fire* in London, 2005.

©*Dave Hogan/Getty Images*

Above right: Robert with his good friends and fellow actors Tom Sturridge and Andrew Garfield at Cecconi's, London, 2009.

©Nick Harvey/*WireImage*

Below: Spotted on location in Central Park filming scenes for *Remember Me* with his on-screen sister Ruby Jerins.

Above left: Robert gives Tai the elephant an affectionate kiss at the *Water for Elephants* press conference in Santa Monica.

©Vera Anderson/Getty Images

Above right: Robert and Katy Perry at the 2010 Teen Choice Awards in California.

©Kevin Mazur/TCA 2010

Below left: With co-stars Taylor Lautner and Kristen Stewart at the premiere of *The Twilight Saga*: *Eclipse* during the 2010 Los Angeles Film Festival.

©Kevin Winter/Getty Images

Below right: Robert attends the *Maps to the Stars* premiere at the 2014 Toronto Film Festival.

©Sarjoun Faour Photography/WireImage

Above: (from left to right) With *Maps to the Stars* cast Martin Katz, Sarah Gadon, Mia Wasikowska, David Cronenburg, Julianne Moore and John Cusack during the 67th Annual Cannes Film Festival, 2014. ©Gareth Cattermole/Getty Images

Below: Robert presents Morten Tyldum with the Hollywood Director Award for *The Imitation Game* at the 18th Annual Hollywood Film Awards, 2014.

©Kevin Winter/Getty Images

Above left: Robert and girlfriend, singer FKA Twigs, in Miami, December 2014.

©Astrid Stawiarz/Getty Images

Above right: Attending the 7th Annual GO GO Gala at Montage Beverly Hills in November 2014. *©Lilly Lawrence/Getty Images*

Below: Heartthrob Rob at the Sydney Film Festival at a photo call for *The Rover*. *©Lisa Maree Williams/Getty Images*

asked how much he had told Rob about Rey he revealed: 'Not a lot. I kept questioning that aspect of it. "What is this economic collapse? I want to know the details about it." Then I realised it didn't really make any difference to my character.'

Rob dismissed the rumours that he was working on an album, which had started because he sings a few lines of 'Pretty Girl Rock' by Keri Hilson in the movie: 'Every few years, something comes out about that. I'm always trying to work on stuff, but I don't know. I'm kind of like, way too sensitive to criticism; I've got enough criticism on one front.'

Rob had felt drawn to projects with small casts because they made him feel like he was creating something himself, rather than just being a small part of a bigger picture. To have his three movies since *Twilight* selected for Cannes made him feel proud, like he was on the right career path and for the first time was being considered a serious actor. Prior to this he had felt that movie critics and the industry as a whole didn't think of him as a talented actor, choosing to dismiss him because of *Twilight*. This had affected his confidence for quite a while, but slowly and surely, it was being boosted, thanks to directors like Cronenberg, Michôd and Corbijn.

The Huffington Post asked Rob what he had learned from the directors he had worked with. He simply replied: 'It's just going to school. I think that's exactly what I'm doing. I think a lot of actors know what they have in them, and they kind of work with directors who help them do the specific thing that they already want. I have no idea what I have! I'm just kind of hoping something will happen if I work with Herzog or Cronenberg.'

He might have managed to tick them off his 'dream directors' bucket list, but he still had quite a few others whom he was desperate to work with. James Gray, director of *We Own the Night* (2007), starring Mark Wahlberg and Joaquin Phoenix, was one such director. Rob had been cast as Henry Costin in his movie *The Lost City of Z* back in November 2013 but he was still waiting for information on when they would be shooting, as the dates kept being pushed back. He was so used to doing things quickly that having to wait was driving him crazy; he literally couldn't wait to hop on a plane to Colombia and get started. He'd been dreaming of working with Gray since he was seventeen.

Rob also wanted to work with the *Spring Breakers*' director Harmony Korine, so had cold-called him and asked to meet up. He confessed to *The Hollywood Reporter*: 'We went to have dinner. He was really nice. But it took me a long time to realise I could do that [cold call directors I wanted to work with].' Rob and Korine got on really well and now consider each other friends. Since they had met up and discussed working together, Korine had been busy writing a movie script for them to collaborate on, but hadn't revealed any of the details to Rob. While waiting to hear, Rob was determined to continue making small movies. He had no desire to become the kind of actor who goes from one big blockbuster to the next until their luck runs out.

For his twenty-eighth birthday Rob decided to go for dinner at Chateau Marmont, Sunset Boulevard. He invited around twenty of his friends to join him and they had a great time. He actually enjoyed himself so much that it took a few days for him to recover.

> **DID YOU KNOW?**
>
> Rob still meets up with some of his *Twilight* co-stars occasionally but it's difficult because they are all busy working on different projects. He tends to play poker with Kellan Lutz, which ends up costing him around $500 a time, because he's by far the worst player.

When he chatted to *The Hollywood Reporter* about his birthday Rob admitted that he'd spent some time chilling on an inflatable chair in a pool, just floating along, drinking rosé, explaining that, 'I literally felt, "This is absolute heaven. This is all I require out of life."'

A few weeks later it was time to release *The Rover* to the wider world. The LA premiere took place Thursday, 12 June 2014 at the Regency Bruin Theatre. Rob had looked extremely handsome in a blue Alexander McQueen suit as he posed for photos with the rest of the cast.

'I'm curious to know whether people who liked the *Twilight* movies will come and see things like *The Rover*,' he admitted to a reporter from the *Telegraph*. 'Hopefully they'll enjoy it. I try to do ambitious projects but I don't know if people are going to like them. You just try and do things which are challenging and hopefully people will appreciate that.'

The Rover received a score of 6.5 out of 10 from IMDb, based on 24,374 reviews. Movie critic Todd McCarthy from *Variety* was impressed when he saw the movie at Cannes and wrote: 'It's a journey that writer-director Michôd, who developed the story with actor Joel Edgerton, uses to explore a multitude of extremes – of desperation, soullessness, viciousness and environmental hostility. If one imagines for a moment that Eric is going to become something resembling a sympathetic protagonist, such notions are dashed the moment he needlessly kills a tough little person who's selling him a gun. The most friendly and humane person to turn up in the entire film, a warm-hearted woman (Susan Prior), who reflexively calls Eric "sweetheart," doesn't last long either after he enters her sphere, and it can fairly be said that the film all but wallows in the squalor of a world in which every human being is viewed with automatic suspicion and where even a smidgen of openness or kindness will not only be perceived as weakness but will be taken advantage of.'

HitFix's Drew McWeeny wasn't taken with the movie's plot but did rate Rob, writing: 'Robert Pattinson's Rey seems like he's barely able to function as a person. He mumbles, he seems like a bit of a dummy, and while he seems capable of violence, he feels like a scared kid who's constantly terrified of everyone else, unsure why people do what they do, unable to communicate on those rare occasions that the synapses all actually do fire. He's very good in the role, and while I'm not crazy about the film as a whole, if Pattinson keeps making choices like this and his ongoing collaboration with David Cronenberg, there may actually be a future for him where people are genuinely shocked to learn that he starred in the "Twilight" movies.'

After *The Rover* premiere it was time to celebrate as the cast, crew and selected guests descended on the W Hotel in Westwood for an exclusive party. *The Fast and the Furious* actress Michelle Rodriguez, *Bad Neighbours'* Zac Efron and Rob's pal Katy Perry were just some of the celebrities invited. The drinks on offer included Loft & Bear cocktails, and for those who were peckish there were sliders, mini pigs-in-a-blanket and chicken skewers to nibble on.

Even though his housing situation had absolutely nothing to do with the movie, journalists couldn't help but mention their surprise that Rob was still renting. They thought that once he had sold the house he once shared with Kristen that he would buy something new straight away but as far as Rob was concerned, he simply hadn't found what he was looking for. He had been so busy filming movies that he hadn't had chance.

He would be concentrating his house search on LA because,

after many years, it finally felt like home. 'I spent two months in England last year, which is the longest I've spent there in six years, which was nice, but I always go back to England at Christmas time and get so depressed that I'm glad to get back to Los Angeles.

'I had this great house, which I bought four or five years ago… It was incredible, absolutely completely crazy. It was like Versailles, with an incredible garden, but I just stayed in one room. I sold it because I suddenly realised I'm not quite old enough to be dealing with plumbing and stuff. So I spent about six months borrowing people's houses, which was nice. Now I'm renting a place which is much smaller,' he confessed to journalist John Hiscock.

Journalists have always been fascinated by how indifferent Rob is to money. Despite having millions in the bank he has remained down-to-earth, his only extravagant purchases being guitars (he has nearly twenty in his collection). He sold his Los Feliz mansion for a cool $6.375 million to *Big Bang Theory* star Jim Parsons (Sheldon Cooper in the hit show) but was happy to bank the money and wait until the right property came along.

When Rob had moved into his rented home in the gated community of Coldwater Canyon he decided not to splash out on furnishing it straight away. He confessed to *The Hollywood Reporter* that he had moved in with three inflatable mattresses and 'this one kind of shitty chair that was left from the previous tenants [in Los Feliz]… I would move my mattresses into different rooms according to the occasion. It was very odd for a while.'

For ages he failed to find which boxes contained his clothes and his DVD collection, saying, 'I don't understand how I don't have any clothes. I've basically stolen every item of clothing that anyone's ever given me for a premiere, but in my closet there's literally about three things.' Rob admitted: 'I was so into [film history] when I was a teenager; I thought it would impress people… but then you get older, and no one gives a shit.'

As well as asking about his house situation journalists also asked about rumours that Rob was potentially going to be the next Indiana Jones. He quickly dismissed the idea that he was going to be taking over from Harrison Ford and said he thinks the people who come up with such rumours are doing it to try and give him lots of bad publicity. 'There will be one totally random article not based on anything, and then there are fifty afterwards totally slamming me,' he told *The Huffington Post*. 'It's like, "I didn't even say anything!"

'It's really crazy [how much false information is published on me]… it's the same stories again and again and again. No matter what. I was trying to figure out a way to not be in tabloids anymore, and I just don't even know how to do it. I thought if you don't get photographed then they can't do anything. [But] no, they put, like, five-year-old photographs in articles.'

Another rumour that had been circulating was that Rob

was dating model Imogen Kerr after they were spotted out and about together a few times. They had been seen together at the 70s-themed Good Times at Davey Wayne's bar in Hollywood in April and then chatting outside the Little Door restaurant, regarded by many as the most romantic restaurant in LA, just a few weeks later. Neither Rob nor Imogen confirmed or denied any relationship but she wasn't at *The Rover* premiere, leaving many fans to believe that the media had once again made the whole thing up.

In the days that followed the premiere some gossip websites tried to suggest that Rob had been getting friendly with Katy Perry at the after-party, and there'd been lots of kissing going on. A few grainy photos of Rob, Katy and some friends chatting were published both online and in print, but all they showed were people smiling and having a good time. To try and 'justify' their claims that something was going on between Rob and Katy some websites decided to republish a video taken many years earlier of the two of them singing karaoke while very drunk.

Katy had told *The Kyle & Jackie O Show* when the video was published first time around: 'That's the media for you. Nothing is sacred, not even karaoke. We were just hanging out, we have a lot of friends that we hang out… one of my best friends is a mutual friend of ours and we got wasted and did karaoke, like people do. About eight years ago and it finally showed up on the Internet!'

DID YOU KNOW?
The song that Rob and Katy sang was Boyz II Men's 'I'll Make Love To You'. The late night karaoke session took place in 2008, so proved that they'd been friends for a long time.

Rob's American fans flocked to cinemas when *The Rover* was released on 13 June but UK fans had to wait until 15 August before they could see it in cinemas. The UK premiere was held at London's BFI Southbank and Rob decided to dress casually in a red suede bomber jacket, a blue shirt and black jeans. He spent half an hour signing autographs for his dedicated fans, who had been waiting hours just to catch a glimpse of him on the red carpet. Many were screaming at the top of their lungs, desperate for him to look in their direction.

When the movie's director David Michôd was interviewed on the red carpet by a reporter from the *Daily Telegraph* he couldn't help but comment on the hysteria Rob faces every single day. 'I feel for him all the time, it's kind of nuts the bubble that he has to live inside. There are kind of very few people in the world who can inspire that sort of bizarre "Beatlemania" and it was one of the extraordinary experiences of working with him out in the desert. It was so freeing for him.

'To be able to sit out in the street with him at the end of the day and drink a beer… it was quite amazing.'

Just over a week later, Rob was at the HFPA Charity

Installation Dinner in Los Angeles to accept a grant on behalf of the American Film Institute alongside *Theory of Everything* actor Eddie Redmayne. The two actors started off their acceptance speech jokingly but turned serious once they started to explain in detail what the American Film Institute does. Rob has always been terrible at reading autocues and was no different on this occasion.

Fans really felt for him when they saw a video of the event, with superfan Black Beanie writing on the *Robsessed* fan site: 'Rob is so not good in these things and Eddy wasn't better either. What is it with these actors who can bring out the deepest emotions in front of a camera and a crew of fifty people but are not able to read from an autocue after a decent introduction? I bet they both died of laughter once they were backstage again, telling each other how terrible they were and then went for a drink. Every time when I read Rob is gonna present somewhere, I wonder how he's gonna screw up this time lol.'

The HFPA (Hollywood Foreign Press Association) gave away almost $2 million worth of grants during the course of the banquet and actors like Morgan Freeman, Elle Fanning, Chris Evans and Kerry Washington were there to accept on behalf of the charities.

HFPA president Theo Kingma told those attending: 'We try every year to give as much as we can to these highly deserving organisations. It is gratifying to know that our efforts are appreciated and we are helping to further the cause of education and film preservation.'

Rob helped another charity, the ALS (Amyotrophic Lateral Sclerosis) Association, on 19 August, when he took part in the Ice Bucket Challenge that was sweeping not only America but the rest of the globe too. It had started on 15 July, when a man called Chris Kennedy from Florida posted up a video on YouTube of himself having a bucket of ice and freezing-cold water poured over him. In the video he challenged three friends in Florida to take part and mentioned the ALS Association because he has a relative who has the condition.

The Ice Bucket Challenge then went viral, with celebrities like Oprah Winfrey, Tiger Woods, Lady Gaga, Tom Cruise and Katy Perry all taking part. Rob had been nominated by Zac Efron and set about doing the challenge even though he didn't have a bucket. He got one friend to pour a pan full of ice cubes onto his head while another jetted him with ice-cold water from a hose. He was so cold, he struggled to speak, and his friends continued to throw ice cubes at him, cups and more water while he revealed that he was nominating Guy Pearce (from *The Rover*), Mia Wasikowska (from *Maps to the Stars*) and Tainted Love singer Marilyn Manson. Rob sent the video to Zac Efron so he could post it up on his YouTube channel to prove that he had done it, as he doesn't have any social media accounts.

At the end of the month Rob jetted to New York to be at the

side of his long-time friend Bobby Long, who was marrying his fiancée, Nicole D'Anna. Rob was a groomsman alongside Sam Bradley, Marcus Foster, Tom Sturridge and a couple more of Bobby's friends.

The timing of the wedding couldn't have been more perfect as he would have been gutted to have missed it if he'd been working. He had a few days off so he could catch up with his friends but then had to fly to Canada as *Maps to the Stars* was having its premiere at the Toronto International Film Festival.

Despite only a few months earlier saying that Los Angeles had become his home and he found spending too much time in London depressing, he told the *Independent* on the day of the premiere: 'I think I need to spend more time in London, or just move around a bit more. I've been in LA for six or seven years and it's weird. The more you stay, especially as an actor, the more you think that you'll be missing out on something by leaving, but you are not really. It's a fun city, but you are permanently on holiday. I feel like I've been on holiday since I was 22.'

He also revealed he was about to change how he approached new projects: 'In the past two years, I've done stuff just for the director and not really thought that much about the script. Now I'm swinging it back a little, trying to get a medium between the two.'

He added: 'Working with Cronenberg just opened stuff up. People approach you in a different way. Now I've done a few other things and it kind of works on a bit of a roll, working with auteur-y guys.'

DID YOU KNOW?
Rob agreed to do *Maps to the Stars* without seeing a script or even knowing anything about the character he was going to play.

Maps to the Stars received a score of 6.4 out of 10 from IMDb, based on 13,832 reviews. But the *Telegraph*'s Robbie Collin couldn't get enough of the movie, awarding it 5 stars out of 5. He confessed: 'My instant reaction, after stumbling, open-mouthed, from the cinema, was a pathological need to stumble back in again. There's so much in this seething cauldron of a film, so many film-industry neuroses exposed and horrors nested within horrors, that one viewing is too much, and not nearly enough. Cronenberg has made a film that you want to unsee – and then see and unsee again.'

Mark Kermode, the *Guardian*'s critic, felt compelled to give it 4 out of 5 stars, writing: 'Beneath the jet-black humour there is real horror – a rampant existential panic that eats away at the lives of the rich and famous, conjuring visions of ghosts from the empty spaces where their souls should be, infecting those who feed upon them and who are desperate to share their disease.'

In November, Rob was due back in Toronto to start filming the movie *Idol's Eye* with Robert De Niro. The *Clouds of Sils*

Maria director Olivier Assayas had been looking forward to working with Rob but alas it wasn't to be. The movie's production company, Benaroya Pictures, closed it down just as filming was about to start.

In a statement they said: 'Due to the criteria for financing not being met by producers, Benaroya Pictures has formally decided to discontinue financing the motion picture titled *Idol's Eye*. The company cannot continue to put its investment at risk and has been forced to stop cash flowing to the production.'

This was a big blow to Rob, Assayas and the rest of the cast, who had all been looking forward to shooting the movie together.

The movie's cancellation gave Rob a couple of weeks off before he was due to present an award to *Headhunters'* director Morten Tyldum at the 2014 Hollywood Film Awards. Rob gets very nervous before presenting at events so would have been feeling under a lot of pressure. Not only were Hollywood's finest going to be there but his ex, Kristen Stewart, would also be there presenting an award to Rob's *Maps to the Stars* co-star Julianne Moore.

On the night itself the press were desperate to get a photo of Rob and Kristen together but Rob knew this well in advance so he decided to skip the red carpet and go straight inside. He didn't want to give journalists and bloggers the opportunity to write stories analysing how they'd 'interacted' on the red carpet.

The next day, some stories did appear but on the whole they

concentrated on the fact that the Chanel dress Kristen was wearing slipped down slightly as she presented her award and revealed more than she would have liked. Rob and Kristen hadn't been spotted speaking to each other so the gossip sites had nothing to go on.

CHAPTER 17

A NEW START

Rob ended 2014 in a new relationship. Some gossip sites might still have been obsessed with writing stories about Rob and Kristen Stewart supposedly pining for each other but he had moved on and was now dating singer Tahliah Barnett, known as FKA Twigs musically and 'Twigs' to her friends. He took her to meet his family over Christmas and they liked her very much.

He had been introduced to Twigs in September of that year by a mutual friend: half-Jamaican, half-Spanish, Tahliah grew up in Gloucestershire before moving to London when she was seventeen. She was given the nickname Twigs because she has joints that crack and she tweeted in August 2014: 'i want to clarify that twigs is not a character that ive created, twigs and Twigs are one and the same. 1 girl, 1 personality, 2 names.'

Unlike anyone Rob had met before, she explained to the *Guardian*'s Tom Lamont: 'I'm an artist, and I'm a bit weird, and I'm probably a bit eccentric.'

Like Rob, she isn't naturally confident when she has to appear on TV shows and when due to perform on the hit US talk show, *The Tonight Show Starring Jimmy Fallon*, she was understandably nervous as 3 million people would be watching at home. However, she didn't want to shy away from the opportunity to impress a new audience and had hired an artist called Daniel Wurtzel to construct an art installation she could move between as she sang – 'It's hard to distinguish yourself… so much could have gone wrong. But I wanted a challenge. I'm at a stage where I want to find things really difficult because now, at this point in my career, it's maybe where some artists sit back on their laurels. Sit back and believe the hype when you haven't actually done anything yet.'

As well as being a talented singer she can also dance and was a dancer in Jessie J's 'Do It Like A Dude' video. She has also danced in videos for Taio Cruz, Ed Sheeran and Kylie Minogue.

Her album, *LP1*, had been released in August 2014 and was well received by critics worldwide. The *Guardian*'s Alexis Petridis had given it 4 out of 5 stars in his review, writing: 'Not many albums sound like *LP1*, a singular piece of work in an overcrowded market. It has its flaws – as you might have intuited from the videos and press shots, they largely stem from trying a bit too hard – but you leave it convinced that FKA Twigs is an artist possessed of a genuinely strong and unique vision, one that doesn't need bolstering with an aura of mystique. Given the times we live in, that's probably just as well.'

Stereogum named it their album of the week and stated: 'Musically, it's hard to even describe what's happening on *LP1*, let alone explain it. The songs have a central pulse to them that feels as natural as breathing, but you don't hear the rhythm in the drums; you hear it in the bass, or the synths, or the way Twigs breathes. The drums echo in from every direction, sounding more like dub-reggae sound effects than like mechanisms for keeping time. Meanwhile, keyboards and voices layer all over each other, creating disorienting fogs. You can get totally lost in your own thoughts listening to these tracks. They seem to fold in on themselves, to make linear thinking difficult.

'There are two singers, Aaliyah and Björk, whose names come up in every *LP1* review, and both are helpful, to an extent. Like Aaliyah, Twigs conveys sex and longing through poise and restraint and timing rather than through loud exhortations or showy technical displays. And like Björk, she's created her entire universe, one that moves her outside any outmoded body/mind or thought/feeling binaries. But Twigs also has a precise, distinctly British locution that reminds me of '80s art-pop types like Kate Bush or Talk Talk's Mark Hollis. And the ease with which she negotiates these tricky, futuristic, altogether alien tracks recalls early Missy Elliott, casually talking s*** over otherworldly Timbaland beats as if that were the most natural thing in the world. All of those comparisons get at little things she does, shades of her style, but none of them is quite right. That because Twigs really sounds like nobody else and belongs to no genre.'

Other critics compared her to music legends Kate Bush and Prince and the album was shortlisted for the Mercury Prize alongside Damon Albarn's *Everyday Robots*, Bombay Bicycle Club's *So Long, See You Tomorrow*, Anna Calvi's *One Breath*, East India Youth's *Total Strife Forever*, Gogo Penguin's *v2.0*, Jungle's *Jungle*, Nick Mulvey's *First Mind*, Polar Bear's *In Each And Every One*, Royal Blood's *Royal Blood*, Kate Tempest's *Everybody Down* and Young Fathers' *Dead*.

The Mercury Prize was judged by a panel of 12 music critics, industry figures, DJs and musicians. They picked Young Fathers' album *Dead* as the winner but Twigs wasn't too disappointed – just making the shortlist was a great achievement. She also found herself nominated for 3 MOBO (Music of Black Origin) Awards in September, but sadly couldn't be in London for the launch as she was filming a video in LA and spending time with Rob.

At the launch, MOBO founder Kanya King MBE told the assembled journalists: 'As we enter our nineteenth year, the MOBO Awards show promises to be bigger and more audacious than ever. This year's nominees represent an incredible crop of artists. I find it particularly exciting to see so many underground artists featured, who've reached new heights over the last year and broken into the wider consciousness.

'It's testament to their talent and their determination to succeed and we are very proud to witness their successes to date. This year's show at Wembley is set to be nothing short of spectacular.'

In the MOBO Best Female Act category, Twigs was up against Jessie J, Katy B, Marsha Ambrosius and Rita Ora and in the MOBO Best Newcomer category she was up against Ella Eyre, Jess Glynne, Kwabs, Little Simz, M.O, Melissa Steel, Meridian Dan, MNEK and Raleigh Ritchie. Her 'Two Weeks' video was up for the MOBO Best Video award, alongside Jacob Banks' 'Move With You', Rudimental ft. Becky Hill's 'Powerless', Scorcher ft. Wretch 32, Mercston & Ari's 'Work Get It' and Skepta ft. JME's 'That's Not Me'. Sadly, she didn't end up winning any of the awards as the Best Female Act award went to Jessie J, Ella Eyre won Best Newcomer and Skepta ft. JME picked up the Best Video award.

When rumours first started circulating that Rob was in a relationship with Twigs, she began receiving abusive messages online. She tweeted on 28 September: 'I am genuinely shocked and disgusted at the amount of racism that has been infecting my [Twitter] account the past week.'

But the abuse didn't make her feel like ending her relationship with Rob because it wasn't his fault and she had spent her life dealing with racism in different forms. In an interview with a French journalist she revealed what her childhood had been like: 'I always felt so separate, so different, I felt like I was in one bubble and everyone else was in another bubble. I remember when I was a chid I was so incredibly sensitive, I was so sensitive if someone was in a bad mood or looked at me funny. I was the only mixed race girl in the whole of my school, and then in the whole of my secondary school and then in my dance school... so obviously, sometimes I just felt... really separate because sometimes I felt like I had no point of reference.'

Fans realised that things were serious between Rob and Twigs when she gave an interview to the *Guardian* in November 2014, in which she admitted that she finds it hard to look at paparazzi photos of them together because she shields her face. She said: 'That side of my life [the paparazzi] is nothing to do with me. That's, like... That is the... side of life of the man that I love. And... when that started happening I had to... Because that is the opposite of who I am as a person, and it was weird... Then I had to sit back and have a conversation with myself and I had to say: that is something really horrible. No, not horrible, I don't find it horrible, it's something that's very challenging. I look uncomfortable because I am uncomfortable. But then it's, like, is this person in my life worth that? And he is, without question. Do you know what I mean? In comparison to how happy I am. And how I feel with him. It's 100 per cent worth it. Does that make sense?'

Rob has always liked to stay out of the limelight as much as possible but from the outset, he was determined that he would support his new girlfriend as she performed shows around the world. He would dress as inconspicuously as possible and try to blend into the crowd, not drawing attention to himself. Most of the time this worked, but occasionally the paparazzi would photograph him watching her perform. They also tried to follow the pair as they went about their daily lives, photographing them coming out of the gym and running simple errands together. Although this was highly irritating for the new couple, it did to confirm to fans that Kristen Stewart was long forgotten. Rob had definitely moved on and seemed to want to spend as much time with Twigs as possible.

Before Rob took Twigs to spend Christmas 2014 with his family, they enjoyed a beach day in Miami together. They had a great time on the beach, catching rays, and seemed completely besotted with each other. Meanwhile they ignored the paparazzi, who seemed determined to take as many pictures as they could of Twigs in her bikini and Rob with his top off.

On arrival in London, Rob didn't just want to introduce Twigs to his family, he introduced her to his friends too. They went out for drinks and she got to meet the people who have been with him through the good and bad times. Because Twigs has been based in London since she was seventeen she too used the opportunity to catch up with her own friends.

At the end of January, Rob had to say goodbye to Twigs for a while and fly to Budapest, Hungary, to shoot the mystery drama *The Childhood of a Leader*. He had been attached to this movie since December 2013 and filming was originally meant to have taken place in May 2014 but had been rescheduled after Juliette Binoche left the project because she felt it was 'too dark'.

The script was written by Brady Corbet and his partner, Mona Fastvold; Corbet was also going to be directing and producing. The movie's themes and plot had been inspired by the 1965 novel *The Magus* by John Fowles and by a short story called *The Childhood of a Leader*, which had been written by the French philosopher and novelist Jean-Paul Sartre and appeared in a collection of short stories published in 1939.

It was a dark tale, set during World War I. Corbet explained to Casey Cipriani from *Indie Wire* in November 2014: 'The film takes place in 1919, it stars a child, it's in French and English. Luckily it's not going to be four-and-a-half hours long and it's not going to be black-and-white. But that's it. It's not a very easy pitch. It's sort of about the birth of a megalomaniac and with a maniacal sort of ego at the turn of the century. It's about the birth of fascism that occurred during the signing of the Treaty of Versailles.

'I have intentionally not revealed the identity of the character. And it's a funny thing because it's not for the reasons that people think. One thing I will happily tell everybody is that the character is not Hitler [laughs]. And the character is not Mussolini. It's someone else. And there's the dramatic event where you learn who this person is and that's something I want to save for people. Robert Pattinson is not playing Hitler as you now know [laughs]. I'll go on the record saying that.'

As soon as Rob finished filming his scenes he jetted off to Germany to be at the 65th Berlin International Film Festival, which was where *Life* was to be shown for the first time on 9 February. Ideally, he would have preferred to arrive a few days earlier as the premiere for *Queen of the Desert* had taken place on 6 February. Rob had missed the opportunity to walk down the red carpet with Nicole Kidman, James Franco and Damian Lewis, which was a real shame but couldn't be helped.

Queen of the Desert received a score of 6.6 out of 10 from IMDb, based on 231 reviews. The *Telegraph*'s Tim Robey titled his review 'Queen of the Desert: Romantic with a great fat capital R' and gave it 2 stars out of 5. He wrote: 'Nicole Kidman does her best, but Werner Herzog's biopic of Gertrude Bell reduces an incredible life to a series of desert vistas and stolen smooches.

'From his first shot, Robert Pattinson, as T.E. Lawrence, is hysterically miscast and bad, but he's also redeemingly cheeky: "Could you please not marry me?" he asks Bell, hoisting up those eyebrows when they catch up for a soul-searching interlude in Petra.

'The film is amusingly top-heavy with its smooching trysts, star power and extravagant desert vistas. The danger of this approach is keeping it up: when Herzog tries to explain the complexity of Bell's career, her unusual influence in imperial policymaking and love of the Arab peoples, that soft, rumbling sound isn't the shifting sands of a world order changing, but merely an audience nodding off.

'His film has the distinction, and also the disadvantage, of being probably the least severe Herzog has yet made: it's pretty and watchable, with Kidman trying her heartfelt best, but it can't make its Gertrude Bell, as lover, cultural pioneer and feminist icon, add up to more than a series of voguish poster-girl poses.'

Peter Bradshaw from the *Guardian* also gave it 2 out of 5 stars: 'Here is the kind of film that you can hardly believe is the work of Werner Herzog who has written and directed it. It is grown-up, respectable and historical, perfectly competently made, lots of accents and period dressing-up … and just the tiniest bit dull.

'Perhaps in flight from her internal emotional turmoil, Bell cultivates her passionate interest in the Bedouin tribesmen and displaces her need for romantic love outwards – into the desert. There she is to encounter Lawrence himself, played boyishly by Robert Pattinson. He looks a little self-conscious in the headdress – though perhaps no more self-conscious than Lawrence himself looked in it. His appearance got a few laughs from the Berlin festival audience, but Pattinson carried off this (minor) role well enough.'

For the *Life* premiere on the 9th, Rob was sporting a full

beard, which was a new look for him and went down well with fans. But the press were less keen, with *Esquire* magazine running a story titled 'How to avoid Robert Pattinson's beard mistake – Bad beard trimming can ruin even one of Hollywood's handsomest faces' the next day. They wrote: 'First it was his hair, and now Robert Pattinson's blowing it in the beard department too. Yesterday, he showed up for the Berlin premier of his new film *Life* sporting a bizarre, pointy leprechaun beard.'

Other magazines and newspapers wrote more serious news pieces about the premiere but the *Metro* seemed keen to suggest that Rob was disinterested on the red carpet. Their story was titled: 'Could R-Pattz BE any less interested in his new film *Life*?'

In their article they said: 'Robert Pattinson showed up at the Berlin International Film Festival premiere for his new movie *Life*, but was he really there? Like really?

'Sure he was sporting a luxurious new beard and a rather dashing suit, but it was something behind the eyes, man.

'Maybe he'd had a bad day, maybe he was missing his other half FKA Twigs, or maybe he was just thinking about his next meal (we feel you on that last one, Rob). Who knows?'

Members of the press were handed production notes before the press conference to give them some background to the movie and these provide a real insight. In the notes Christina Piovesan, one of the producers, described how well director

Anton Corbijn and Rob worked together to make his portrayal of Dennis Stock as convincing as possible. She said: 'I remember seeing him [Corbijn] talking to Rob in the dark room where he, as Stock, is developing the iconic photo of James Dean in Times Square. Anton was guiding Rob through that scene and he was just so animated and seemed to feel so at home in that dark room. It was exciting to see how he was communicating his passion [for photography] to Rob.'

Rob confessed: 'A few months before production, I started shooting on the same Leica that Stock had. There's something quite gentle about it compared to digital photography because you can't force a picture. You can't shoot as if you're on an iPhone and just put a filter on it afterwards.' He had wanted to be as authentic as possible and had spent time visiting the Leica photography office in London for tips before shooting began. Their expert tuition had given him the tools to be able to take better photos but he didn't become a master overnight, 'it takes a long time to be able to take even okay pictures, let alone good ones.'

Iain Canning, another of the movie's producers, was extremely impressed by his dedication, stating: 'In embodying the role, Rob has grappled with how important it is to understand the emotional dynamics of Dennis at the time, to understand that it was an era whereby men of twenty-seven were expected to have settled down, to be living a certain life, and Dennis Stock wasn't living that life.'

In the notes, Rob admits that he was first attracted to the project because it was 'an interesting period in history and an interesting take on such a massive character as James Dean... I read the script for quite a long time before I decided to do it.

'I liked that Dennis Stock is written as being quite a bad dad. Regardless of the period or of James Dean, in a movie you don't normally see a guy who had a kid pretty young and thinks it's restricting his life as an artist, or whatever it is that he wants to be, and is very open about it. It's quite frankly dealt with in the script.

'The idea of having a seven-year-old kid is interesting for me. That doesn't happen very often for people my age.'

Rob was also interested in the role because he would be co-starring with an actor his own age, but he wanted to make sure that the right person was cast: 'My decision was so dependent on who was playing Jimmy.' He didn't want someone to be given the part just for looking like James Dean and was thrilled when Dane DeHaan was cast.

Anton Corbijn liked how different Rob and Dane were, as actors and as people, because he felt this worked well, considering the characters they were playing in the movie were very different too – 'You can imagine they could be friends because they're different and that's interesting in friendships – you offer the other person something that they don't have,' he revealed.

Dane DeHaan commented: 'I really respect Rob's bravery in

jumping into films like this. He continues to challenge himself as an artist, and I'm glad I could go on this particular journey with him.'

During the press conference, Rob admitted that he hadn't seen the movie, despite the screening being the night before. He revealed: 'I actually didn't watch it last night... Because after Cannes I literally I got so... I feel like I lost a few years of my life watching a screening, just sitting there with your heart just wrenching inside your chest. I just can't do it anymore so I'm going to watch it like, probably tomorrow. So yeah, I don't know what the reaction is. I'm just kind of, in a trance the entire time, but yeah, it seemed like people appreciated it. There was a nice applause and stuff.'

He can never avoid *Twilight* questions and before filming began was asked by one journalist whether he'd had any idea of what the reality of fame was going to be like. Rob replied: 'I don't know what I thought it was going to be. I mean, it's weird, I still feel like I'm doing the same stuff. I mean, I guess up until *Twilight* I was really just auditioning for absolutely everything and just trying to get anything so I guess that's a sort of different career but I mean, afterwards it's so rare that I find anything not only that I like but that I feel like I can add something to or do at all, so it's really trying to find anything to do.

'It always surprises me when a script comes and I'm like, "oh!" I just signed onto this thing *Brimstone* – it's just a small

part in something but I was so surprised that this part that…
Like I really, really had an idea of how to do it and I'm always
like, "Oh, where has this idea come from?" I'm always surprised
that I had any idea at all so yeah, it's kind of a strange career.'

He admitted that his fans have calmed down quite a bit from
his *Twilight* days – 'I used to be, I used to just let it really, really
get to me and I've kind of become a lot more calm recently. Also,
I've spent more time in London and it's completely different in
London. It's like, if someone asks for a photo in London and
you say "no", it's not like…. A lot of the time, in L.A. especially,
people are like "Why?" You know, like: "Really? You want me
to explain why? I'll just do a photo, then." In London, people
don't really so it's kind of different but yeah, it definitely has
calmed down.'

Rob was then asked where he'd like to be in 10 years' time
and this was something he didn't wish to divulge. He did say,
however, 'In the next few years I know just after last year like,
two of my movies kind of, one fell apart and the other one got
pushed to this year and I ended up like, kind of just waiting
for a job for ages and I was just like, "okay, I need to be, I'm
never having a year like that again. I'm going to be a lot more
prolific in my productivity rate". Cause I think it's suddenly
getting up to 30 as well and you're just like "argh! I need to
do loads of stuff!" So I'm definitely going to be much more
productive.'

Life received a score of 7.1 out of 10 from IMDb, based

on 144 reviews. But the *BBC*'s Nicholas Barber was less than impressed, awarding it a measly 2 stars out of 5. He wrote: 'The casting is perverse. Pattinson, with his long-chinned handsomeness, would seem to be an ideal Dean, while DeHaan is best known as the glowering, round-faced supervillain in *Chronicle* and *The Amazing Spider-Man 2*, but they both make a decent fist of their counter-intuitive roles. Pattinson has all the fidgety resentfulness of a man who is impatient to be given his due, and DeHaan's high-pitched mumble and gravity-defying quiff are passably Dean-ish.

'However, both actors are so weighed down with weariness that they can barely keep their heads from slumping forward onto their chests. Again and again, the sullen Stock announces that he wants to create groundbreaking art, but his main method of doing so is to stand around and mope. Even when he is with Dean, sparks refuse to fly. All that happens is that the pair of them mope together, as if they are perpetually trudging through the mist and rain. There's just not much life in *Life*; Stock's actual pictures of Dean have a verve and spontaneity that Corbijn's slow, studied drama is lacking.

'The film's fundamental flaw, though, is that we were right all along: as iconic as it might be, that shot of Dean in Times Square came about when Stock stood in front of him and clicked the shutter, and there's not much more to it than that. Luke Davies's screenplay attempts to lend the men's brief, uneventful acquaintance some deeper significance: Dean learns that there is no place like home, and Stock learns that he should stay in New York and be a father to his son. But those aren't the most earth shattering of lessons. When your hero's big epiphany is that he should stop vomiting on children, you may not have a story to tell.'

Peter Bradshaw from the *Guardian* also awarded the movie 2 out of 5 stars: 'Opposite DeHaan is Robert Pattinson playing photographer Dennis Stock, whose persistence and determination got these great shots. Sadly, Pattinson's natural style and charisma is suppressed, perhaps because Dean is supposed to be the charismatic one, but we are given little or nothing to show Stock's watchful, non-starry ordinariness. It's a frankly flat and unengaged performance from Pattinson, and there is no real tension or chemistry between the two men. I would like to have seen Pattinson being his own saturnine power to the role of Dean – I even found myself wondering if DeHaan and Pattinson could not somehow change and change about in the course of the film, like Jonny Lee Miller and Benedict Cumberbatch in Danny Boyle's famous stage production of *Frankenstein*.

'At one stage, Dean tells his uncle that Stock is a typical New Yorker: "prickly, pushy and opinionated". Really? He mostly seems like a quiet, polite guy with not much to say for himself. As for Dean, DeHaan's performance has confidence and self-possession, and he has a real charisma of his own. But he gives us little or nothing of what might lie behind these licensed and approved images. There are some pleasing touches, but this film is a frustrating experience.'

Once he had finished promoting *Life* it was back to Los Angeles to do two days of photo shoots. A fan called Choy Brown got to meet him, tweeting: 'Just literally ran into Robert Pattinson doing a photo shoot. Didn't see the whole crew right there watching him take off his coat.'

Another fan called Beth tweeted a pic of Rob by a bike, looking very sexy and the message: 'This handsome (man) was in today by my work! I'm so lucky!! #RobertPattinson.'

On 23 February Rob attended the Oscars in a midnight blue suit. Afterwards he got to let his hair down at the Vanity Fair Oscar Party at the Wallis Annenberg Center in Beverly Hills, California. He enjoyed spending time with his close friend Tom Sturridge and his fiancée, actress Sienna Miller. Twigs couldn't be there with him because she was preparing for the BRIT Awards on the 25th at the O2 Arena in London. During the course of the night, Rob was able to catch up with a whole host of other famous faces as Jay Z, Beyoncé, Reese Witherspoon, Emma Stone and Miley Cyrus were also in attendance.

In their write-up of the event *Vanity Fair* shared: 'Robert Pattinson, unable to move through the crowd, jumped over an ottoman to meet a friend—all, impressively, without spilling his beer. And, in perhaps our favorite grouping of the evening, Benedict Cumberbatch spent part of the night deep in conversation with Joan and Jackie Collins over french fries.

'Cigarette girls in vintage-inspired designs passed out retro candy and Cracker Jack caramel popcorn. And each of the 150 dinner guests invited to view the ceremony while feasting on a sumptuous dinner from chef Thomas Keller were gifted a zippo lighter with a quote from Hollywood's ancestral screen siren Mae West: "You only live once, but if you do it right, once is enough".

> **DID YOU KNOW?**
> Many people believed that Rob deserved to have been nominated for the Best Supporting Actor award for his portrayal of Rey in *The Rover* but alas, it wasn't to be.

Twigs will always be dedicated to her music but if she could have been with Rob at the Oscars then she would have done so. She wants to support him whenever she can, and he feels exactly the same about her. He felt immensely proud when he found out that she'd been nominated for the Female Solo Artist and British Breakthrough awards at the BRITs. She was given the honour of performing a mash-up of 'Hide' and 'Pendulum' at 'The BRITs Are Coming' nominations launch in January 2015, which had been an amazing opportunity for her. Other performers that day had been Jessie Ware, who sang 'You &

I (Forever)', Clean Bandit & Jess Glynne, who performed a mash-up of 'Real Love' and 'Rather Be', and James Bay, who sang 'Let It Go'.

Photographers snapping the artists on the red carpet for the actual awards show itself on the 25th didn't think that Rob had decided to support Twigs at the event as she appeared on her own but he certainly was there, out of sight. It was her night and had they shared the red carpet all eyes would have been on him. Twigs looked stunning in an eye-catching Alexander McQueen outfit. The *Daily Mail*'s Lucy Mapstone wrote in her fashion round-up: 'The top half of the singer's eye-catching Alexander McQueen ensemble was styled in a strappy, harness-like affair in velvet, showing off her slender waistline and giving a peek at her side-boob.

'While her outlandish get-up would have looked odd on another, the British singer's petite and athletic frame and striking looks carried it off flawlessly.

'To balance out the revealing nature across her chest and torso, FKA Twigs – whose real name is Twigs Debrett Barnett – covered the wide-legged trousers of her outfit with a long black and white swathe of decorated fabric.

'She added to her eye-catching look with her hair in her trademark long braids, some of them gathered and curled on top of her head.'

Rob would have loved it had she won both of her nominated awards but it wasn't to be. In the Female Solo Artist category she was up against Ella Henderson, Jessie Ware, Lily Allen and Paloma Faith. Presenter Mark Ronson called out the winner as being Paloma Faith. The British Breakthrough category was presented by Radio 1 host Fearne Cotton and singer-songwriter Charli XCX. In this category, she was up against Chvrches, George Ezra, Royal Blood and Sam Smith. The award went to Sam Smith, who had already performed his track 'Lay Me Down' earlier on in the show and would go on to win the biggest award of the night, the BRITs Global Success.

Despite not winning an award Twigs still had a great night, sitting with Rob and enjoying some great performances from the likes of Taylor Swift, Ed Sheeran, Kanye West, George Ezra and the Queen of Pop, Madonna. The 2015 awards would go down in history as the one where Madonna was dragged backwards down a flight of stairs. Twigs thankfully didn't suffer any wardrobe malfunction of her own and partied with Rob at the Warner Music after-party. Former Pussycat Dolls singer Ashley Roberts revealed to ITV2: 'Her [FKA Twigs] and Robert Pattinson was getting quite sexy, they were right in front, giving me a good old show.

'They are feeling very much in love, I think.'

The next day many magazines commented on how loved-up Rob and Twigs were, publishing blurry photos of them together at the party. In the majority of the photos, Rob is captured looking at Twigs with a huge grin on his face and they seem like any other young couple in love. He didn't have any immediate acting jobs to do so for a while he was going to be hitting the road with Twigs in March and supporting her on a tour of Europe. They would enjoy some time together in Paris and Amsterdam, before and after the shows.

In April, Rob was heading to Coachella, the annual music and arts festival where he used to go with Kristen Stewart to celebrate her birthday. This time around he was with Twigs and she was going to be performing on stage.

His good friend Katy Perry was also there and joined Rob as they watched Twigs entertain her audience. They spent time chatting and enjoying the other acts, with Rob and Twigs happily interacting with fans the next day as they enjoyed the rest of the festival together.

The press were keen to get as many photos of the couple as they could as the news that they were engaged had been announced less than two weeks earlier. The person credited with letting the cat out of the bag was Twigs' friend and collaborator T-Pain.

T-Pain is an American singer-songwriter and record producer who has worked with the likes of Kanye West, Jamie Foxx and Flo Rida. He actually credits Twigs with changing his life, telling *Fader*: 'It's been great [working with FKA Twigs], man. It's been a whole different experience. Twigs actually changed my whole perspective on the music industry. She made me proud of myself again, the way she was talking to me.

'I told her I wanted to do some stuff, like videos and put out some songs. But I was like, "I can't." She was like "Why?" I was like, "You know, the label and stuff like that." She was like, "Why? Do they control you? How are they controlling you? What, are they gonna sue you? Cause that's their money, too." [Laughs] She opened my eyes. I felt like I was brainwashed and she came and reset me. Like, "Why am I not putting out songs? Why am I not doing this?" Cause every time I see her, there's a new video, a new song. I'm like, "Your label's okay with that?" And she's like, "I don't give a f*** about that" [laughs]. It changed my life, you know, the way she looked at things, and I tell her every time I talk to her. She changed my life. It was amazing.'

He hadn't wanted to upset Twigs but during an interview with *Vulture* on 1 April he had been asked if she would appear on his new album. Without thinking, he replied: 'Well, the first time we even met each other, we met in the studio. Her music's changed a lot since then. But she's on tour so much, and anytime I call her, she's in a different place. And she's engaged now, so that's about to be a whole other thing.'

When the journalist remarked: 'Wait, she's engaged? That's news to me.'

He replied: 'Yeah, to ol' Patty [Robert Pattinson]. I don't know if she wanted anybody to know that…'

He tried to suggest that he had said they were engaged as a joke, tweeting a picture of two rings and the message: 'Added a little #AprilFools to my interview with @vulture today!' but

People magazine later confirmed the news that Rob and Twigs were engaged after six months of dating. Their source said that they were inseparable and were living together at Rob's house (when Twigs wasn't away touring, of course).

In the weeks and months to follow magazines and newspapers printed stories from various 'sources' claiming to have the lowdown on their wedding plans. Some 'insiders' claimed that Twigs wanted an informal pub wedding but Rob preferred a traditional church wedding in the summer, while others suggested that Twigs had banned all members of the *Twilight* cast – which seemed a little far-fetched to many fans. Obviously, fans didn't expect Kristen Stewart to get an invite but they couldn't see why everyone else would be excluded unless the couple were opting for a small, intimate wedding.

Nikki Reed, who played Rosalie Cullen in the *Twilight* movies, told *Yahoo* in April: 'I'm the biggest fan [of FKA Twigs]. I'm a true fan. It's so rad that she's with my co-star because I'm a true fan of her. I'm going to ask him if he can get an autograph for me. She's such an amazing musician. She's an artist through and through. She's a true artist and always has been.'

In May, Rob had to say a temporary goodbye to Twigs and get back to work as he was playing a character called Samuel in Martin Koolhoven's thriller *Brimstone*. At Koolhoven's request details of his character were kept a secret from the press, with the only information shared being that he was some kind of outlaw.

Brimstone would see Rob reunite with two actors he had worked with before: Guy Pearce (Eric in *The Rover*) and Mia Wasikowska (Agatha in *Maps to the Stars*). Guy was to play the Reverend and Mia would play the female lead, Liz. They were to be joined by *Game of Thrones* actress Carice van Houten and filming was to take place in Canada and Europe.

The movie's financer, Embankment, released a statement in February 2015, in which their co-founder Tim Haslam said: 'Wasikowska is a powerhouse performer. Guy Peace plays a hunter who unleashes hell. Martin directs a highly emotional, gripping and unique story of a mesmerising woman who battles the vengeance of a zealot.'

The *Embankment* website also revealed the movie's synopsis:

'Retribution is coming…

'Prepare yourself. For something very special…

'A triumphant epic of survival set in the searing wilds of the Badlands, the menacing inferno of the old American West.

'A tale of powerful womanhood and resistance against the unforgiving cruelty of a hell on earth.

'Our heroine is Liz, carved from the beautiful wilderness, full of heart and grit, accused of a crime she didn't commit, hunted by a vengeful Preacher – a diabolical zealot and her twisted nemesis.

'But Liz is a genuine survivor; she's no victim – a woman of fearsome strength who responds with astonishing bravery to claim the better life she and her daughter deserve.

'Fear not. Retribution is coming.'

Director Koolhoven couldn't wait to work with Rob, as he had been so impressed with his performance as Rey in *The Rover*. The character he would be playing in *Brimstone* was completely different but Koolhoven knew he would do a great job. He revealed to *Veronica* magazine (translated from Dutch to English): 'Pattinson was a teen-idol. A lot of fans are still very loyal. I didn't know he was that popular. I knew he was popular, but not that there are people that have more or less devoted their lives to finding every bit of news about him on the internet, so every interview and most probably also this one – "hello, Pattinson fans" – will be translated and then everybody talks about it. And because I am on Twitter they tag my name so my whole Twitter-feed is full.

'He has a kind of rebellious charisma and he is a handsome guy and he is a very good actor. So I believe he is going to be really good.'

For Rob to be away from her while he filmed the movie was hard for Twigs. She talked to *The New York Times* about what it was like to date someone as famous as him and receive abuse online: 'It's really hard – I can't begin to explain how awful it is… It makes you want to just stop everything sometimes. It makes you want to smash your face into the mirror.'

When describing the racist tweets and messages she receives she said: 'It's relentless… There's no amount of songs I can sing or dances I can dance that will prove to them I'm not a monkey.'

Despite all the abuse, nothing will stop her from loving Rob with all her heart: 'I'm so happy, I didn't see my life going this way at all, but it's worth it.'

She enjoys every moment they spend together, in private and in front of the cameras at events such as the Met Gala, which was held at the beginning of May before Rob had to leave for *Brimstone*. That night, they lit up the red carpet, with Twigs wearing a colourful Christopher Kane gown (adorned with erotic naked body parts) and Rob looking dapper but slightly more conservative in a black suit. He seemed so happy with his arm around Twigs, smiling for the cameras and showing the world that he was with his soulmate.

At the time of writing Rob has some great movies lined up for the rest of 2015. Filming for *The Lost City of Z* is due to start, a project that he was first associated with in November 2013. Back then, Benedict Cumberbatch was due to play the lead role of explorer Percy Fawcett but dropped out in 2014 because of scheduling conflicts with Marvel's *Doctor Strange*. His part will now be taken by Charlie Hunnam, while Rob's friend Sienna Miller will play Percy's wife Nina. Rob's role is that of Henry Costin, Fawcett's assistant. The director is James Gray and the movie will be produced by Brad Pitt, Dede Gardner, Jeremy Kleiner, Dale Johnson and Anthony Katagas.

The film is based on a 2009 non-fiction book of the same title written by the American journalist David Grann. The plot centres around Percy Fawcett, a British surveyor in the 1920s who disappears in the Amazon jungle with his companions while searching for a mythical city. It's set to be released in 2016.

It is also thought that Rob will be in a movie called *The Trap*, which is due to be released in 2017. The plot is top-secret at the present time, however what is known is that it centres on a crime family in the American South. Other actors rumoured to be starring in the project include Idris Elba, Al Pacino and James Franco. The director is Harmony Korine, one of Rob's heroes.

So, what does the future hold for Rob? Will his relationship with Twigs stand the test of time? So far they seem as solid as can be, both equally besotted. To get engaged after only six months might seem like a rush to some people, but others can appreciate that once you know, you know.

Rob has been a worldwide star since *Twilight* hit cinemas in November 2008 but fame hasn't changed him. He might have picked up more than thirty awards, but he's still the boy from Barnes, looking for his next acting adventure. He'll always be the type of actor who doesn't want to do the norm; he doesn't want to settle for movies that don't have a message for the world. So, will we see him win an Oscar one day? His fans certainly hope so!

Above all, Rob never wants to be bored. He still has a list of directors he admires, with whom he would like to work in the future, and he'd love to stand at the other side of the camera as a producer or director too. He has always said he'd like a family one day but right now he is just so busy that the chances of this happening any time soon seem unrealistic. As he reaches the end of his twenties, his fans can't wait to see what the next decade has in store for him.